THE WAY OF MODERNISM
& OTHER ESSAYS

T0382311

The
WAY OF MODERNISM
& OTHER ESSAYS

BY

J. F. BETHUNE-BAKER
D.D., F.B.A.
Lady Margaret's Professor
of Divinity, Cambridge

CAMBRIDGE
AT THE UNIVERSITY PRESS
1927

CAMBRIDGE
UNIVERSITY PRESS

University Printing House, Cambridge CB2 8BS, United Kingdom

Cambridge University Press is part of the University of Cambridge.

It furthers the University's mission by disseminating knowledge in the pursuit of
education, learning and research at the highest international levels of excellence.

www.cambridge.org
Information on this title: www.cambridge.org/9781107450967

© Cambridge University Press 1927

First published 1927
First paperback edition 2014

A catalogue record for this publication is available from the British Library

ISBN 978-1-107-45096-7 Paperback

NOTE

All the papers included in this volume have been used as lectures or addresses of one kind or another. Some of them have already been printed in the *Modern Churchman* and I am indebted to the Editor of that journal for leave to reprint them. In one of them, 'Evolution and Christian Theology', I have taken over a page or two of a review of the book *Evolution in relation to Modern Knowledge* contributed to the *Edinburgh Quarterly Review* for January 1926. In printing the others I am complying with the wish of some of those who heard them, or have read them since they were delivered. I am encouraged to publish them in the hope that, read together, they may be found to offer a way of approach for our own generation to that synthesis of old ideas and new knowledge which has been the aim of 'modernism' in all ages, and I have kept the personal form of address.

I am not able to speak or write on any of the subjects dealt with in this volume without reflecting the point of view which, with the growing experience of life, I have found increasingly satisfying to mind and heart and will. There are, therefore, in the various papers written at different times some repetitions even of illustrations. These seem to be required in their places and may, I hope, be pardoned.

J. F. B-B.

23 *August*, 1927

CONTENTS

§ I

THE WAY OF MODERNISM[1]

'Modernism' and 'modernist' are terms that have been freely bandied about for the last twenty or thirty years. To some they imply something destructive of Religion, to others all that is enlightening and progressive and of best promise for the future of mankind.

While I was hesitating as to the choice of a subject for this paper, I lighted on an article in a recent number of one of the best French theological periodicals with the title 'The Legacy of Modernism'.[2] This seemed to suggest that the time had come to write an obituary notice of a movement that was now defunct. I soon found that this was not the idea of the author of the article. He knows that though the movement was officially killed for all who admit the authority of the Vatican, it is still very much alive; and, being a member of the faculty of Protestant Theology in the University of Strasbourg, he sets himself to consider its effects on Protestantism in general and the points, so to say, at which Protestantism not only can, but ought to, come to terms with it and amend its traditional conceptions accordingly.

I am not going to give a *résumé* of this article, which is probably too technical for our purposes tonight. But I am prompted by it to try to give some kind of

[1] A paper read to a College Theological Society in 1924.
[2] A. N. Bertrand 'L'héritage du modernisme' *Revue d'histoire et de philosophie religieuses* iv 4 (July–Aug. 1924).

review of the movement which may be a reminder to those who have lived through some of its acutest phases (if it be a disease) or its most creative moments (if we take a kindlier view of it), and may also help others, for whom 'modernism' and 'modernist' are words of little meaning, to place themselves in regard to them. So it is a historical sketch that is wanted first.

If I were to begin at the beginning, as I conceive the movement, I should have to go back to the enterprising being in prehistoric times who diverged from the ways of the common ancestors of the anthropoid ape and man. Then, coming down to times of which we have more evidence, I should be able to pick out modernists in social polity and morality and science and literature and art all down the ages. In the more limited history with which we are specially concerned, namely, that of the Christian Society and the Christian Religion, I should find modernists from the beginning conspicuous on the pages of that varied and interesting history. I forbear to give you my selection, lest the list of names should seem to prejudice the calm and cool consideration of the matter which we want.

But we cannot consider the matter at all without looking back to the past. For though the modernism we have to deal with is an ecclesiastical and theological phenomenon of the last thirty years only, its roots go much farther back. They go back in the sphere of Biblical criticism at least as far as the English Deists of the eighteenth century, whose influence passed through Bolingbroke and his friendship with Voltaire to France, and on to Germany—coming back to England, all the stronger for being a little humanized, in the middle of last century. In other spheres roots are to be found in the new methods, and the new knowledge of nearly all studies outside the ecclesiastical domain, which were first systematically and almost universally followed and disseminated in the nineteenth century, especially in history and anthropology and all the physical sciences. In Germany, in France, in England, to some extent in Switzerland and in Italy, students of the Christian Tradition began to study their history with eyes opened to the results obtained by students in the field of secular things. Always at one point or another they found themselves in conflict with the Tradition.

So, too, new philosophies more or less dependent on the new views of the universe came into existence from the time of Descartes in the seventeenth century and put the philosophical basis of the Church system into a position of isolation from current thought.

Modernism stands out perhaps most clearly as a new method; 'system' it never has been: a method intended to find a way by which all the knowledge of the day could be legitimatized in the Church.

To anyone who wants to study the recent history of the movement in detail I would warmly commend Archdeacon Lilley's review of it (*Modernism: a record and review*, Pitman and Sons, 1908). Having followed this history myself through its different stages and read the writings of leading representatives of its various phases, I have been much indebted to Archdeacon Lilley's book in preparing this paper and have used some of his language. If my borrowings send you to his book, so much the better.

1-2

Modernism, then, in its technical sense, as he deals with it, is a current of thought which became conspicuous in the Catholic Church towards the end of last century. It became widespread among the French clergy and some laymen both in England and in France; it ranged over the whole field of theological studies. We may pick out three aspects in particular of the whole problem to which it was directed, each of which has its representative exponent: the problem of Dogma or the problem of Truth, the problem of the relation between History and Faith, the problem of Authority.

In all cases the chief writers hoped to establish a concordat between Tradition and the new knowledge and new spirit of the time. Their work was warmly welcomed by many of their *confrères*: by others attacked as implying and leading to the dissolution of the Church and the Christian Religion. One after another the chief books were condemned by the papal authorities and finally the whole movement by a papal decree (3 July 1907, *Lamentabili sane exitu*) and a papal encyclical (7 Sept. 1907, *Pascendi dominici gregis*).[1]

The first of these papal documents recites sixty-five propositions said to be actually contained in the writings under review. Latin lends itself to epigrammatic expression, and many of these sixty-five propositions are too brief and crude in statement to represent at all adequately the teaching which they profess to summarize. They are all condemned as *errores modernistarum*. And the long encyclical which

[1] See H. Denzinger (C. Bannwart) *Enchiridion Symbolorum* pp. 538 ff. (B. Herder, 1913).

followed two months later reasserted 'in its most relent-less form the conception of Religion as mere submission to a closed and rigid system'[1]—the traditional system, that is, of the Church of Rome and the philosophy of Thomas Aquinas, all speculation since his time being scornfully dismissed as 'ravings of philosophers'. The error of modernists is said to be a step farther from the error of Protestants on the way to Atheism.

Three years later (1 Sept. 1910) this encyclical was followed by an oath against the errors of modernism, issued by the Pope on his own initiative, which all professors and teachers in universities, colleges, and schools were required to take. It is an elaborate affirmation of all the traditional points of view and a definite reprobation of the newer conceptions which characterize the modernist position.

In Germany, where the universities were in receipt of grants from the State, the Government intervened to save its Roman Catholic scholars from the in-dignity of having to repudiate the methods and results of free historical investigation; but elsewhere, I under-stand, the oath has been administered and taken. It was regarded, I believe, as belonging to the sphere of administration and discipline. It marks the official burial of the corpse of modernism by the Church of Rome; and there, for the time being, the history of Roman Catholic modernism ends.

As no other Churches have the same organization, even if such governing bodies as there are may not be lacking in will, no such fate has befallen them. Students who are working in them on lines similar to

[1] Lilley *op. cit.* p. 263.

5

those condemned by Rome can do so with a fair measure of toleration, though 'modernist' is of course a term of evil significance to many religious people.

I have said it is a very vague term. I am not sure, but I believe it was first coined by the enemy—affixed as a label to the new ideas which they did not like; the Catholic Church has always been officially opposed to every novelty as long as it was a novelty. But in less conservative circles it is not necessarily a term of reproach, and in England at all events it is not uncommon now to hear modernists charged with arrogance for using of themselves a name which seems to imply that they are the only people who are up-to-date, while everyone else is behind the times.

What then is it all about? Let me recur first to the three aspects mentioned already.

1. The problem of Dogma or of Truth.

Here a chief exponent of the new point of view is Le Roy[1]—a philosopher of distinction of the school of Bergson and Boutroux, a professing and practising Catholic, whose avowed aim was to elucidate the idea of dogma and to explain how it was to be reconciled with freedom of speculative research.

What he has in view is the traditional conception of dogma as a truth given on external authority, or else dependent on 'proofs' which have no such demonstrative validity as is claimed for them, and further

[1] Art. 'What is a Dogma?' published in the French *Fortnightly* 16 Apr. 1905: republished with replies to the objections taken to it by various bishops and others of the clergy and further explanation and exposition of his argument as *Dogme et Critique* 1907.

6

expressed in language which is sometimes that of a philosophic system no longer understood and sometimes that of metaphors borrowed from common life and capable of various meanings—so that the dogma to which intellectual assent is required is unintelligible, and no one can be certain what it is that it affirms and denies, inasmuch as imaginative symbols and abstract formulae are mixed together in the statement of it.

To shew how unsatisfactory this intellectualist conception of dogma is he takes three instances: the dogmas of the Personality of GOD, of the Resurrection of Jesus, and of the Real Presence. If dogmas are regarded as conveying truths of the speculative or theoretic order, none of these selected dogmas will bear examination. The terms used in them—Personality, Resurrection, Presence—must all be given meanings for which we have no intellectual equivalents. They do not express a precise rational concept.

This idea of dogma must therefore be abandoned. The most that can be claimed for it on the intellectual side is a negative sense or value. In the illustrations he takes, no positive information, no explicit idea, is given about GOD, the Resurrection, the Sacramental Presence. But the first dogma tells us that GOD is not impersonal, as a law or formal category or principle, or abstract entity, or universal substance, or any kind of cosmic force pervading everything—it warns us against various forms of pantheism. The dogma of the Resurrection teaches nothing about the mechanism or the manner or kind of the second life of Jesus, but it excludes some conceptions as that death had put an end to the action of Jesus on

7

the things of this world, so that He no longer had any part in our life, or had it only as a thinker whose influence still remained lively and productive, and of whose work effects could still be found. It says that death was not for Him, as it is for the generality of men, the definite end of practical activity. Similarly, though the doctrine of the Real Presence does not define the presence, yet it does say that it must not be thought of merely symbolically or figuratively.

But Le Roy does not stop here. The consideration of the merely negative sense of dogma on the intellectual plane leads on to the thesis that the true use of dogma is to direct that practical knowledge which is the only knowledge with which religion is concerned. A dogma is a rule of practical conduct. So the dogma of the Personality of GOD says to us in effect: 'Conduct yourselves in your relations with GOD as you would in your relations with a human person'. The dogma of the Resurrection of Jesus says: 'Be in relation to Him as you would have been before His death, as you are to a contemporary of your own'. And the dogma of the Real Presence enjoins on us an attitude of spirit such as we should feel in the presence of Jesus Himself if He were visible to us. Such rules of practical conduct may rightly be imposed by the Church which is above all else the generalized tradition of the highest religious experience. It cannot impose a speculative truth on the reason of man, but it is its function to direct conduct and the religious life. And when we view dogmas from this angle we see their constant and abiding character, so that in different ages and at different levels of intellectual culture they make the same appeal, just because human nature itself and practical life in the world are in their fundamental interests and experiences uniform.

That, then, is the conception of dogma which this French Catholic philosopher puts forward as against the intellectualist view that dogmas are revelations of speculative truth. The account which I have given is very incomplete. I have tried only to seize on main features. It has as its basis the author's philosophy of the primacy of action, of life lived, over thought. It insists that religion is not theology, but that theology grows out of religion; and that, I think, is the conception that underlies modern thought on the subject. It means, of course, that all theological formulas must be tested by their correspondence with religious experience, that their values are not speculative but practical.

Apart from any definite scheme of philosophy, the claim has been made that we should concentrate our attention on *the religious construction* of all our traditional doctrines: that we should be regarded as pledged, when we affirm them, not to belief in the intellectual propositions they plainly set before us, or the particular happenings or facts of history which they assert or imply, but to the values or meanings for conduct and the attitude to life which those particular beliefs conveyed or expressed for the men of old who had them.[1]

To me it seems that this is the only way in which we can reconcile our traditional system of theology with modern knowledge and thought. If we follow this way we part company from our forefathers as to

[1] I have tried to expound this point of view in *The Faith of the Apostles' Creed* (Macmillan, 1918).

9

beliefs about many things which were the basis, or the framework, of their doctrines. Now and again we may have to repudiate a doctrine. But in general we are able to make the same affirmations of faith which they connected with their particular formulations of fact.

The issue becomes clearer when we turn to the second of the three problems which are prominent in modernist writings.

2. The problem of the relation between History and Faith.

This problem arises from the eager study of early Christian literature and origins and institutions of the Church which was carried on last century in Germany in particular though by no means exclusively. The position, I suppose, is too familiar to need many words of description. The study of secular literature and history had led to many conclusions very different from received opinion about that literature and history. It had shewn that the names attached to ancient writings were not always those of their actual authors and that history had often been written more with an eye to edification than to accurate narrative of fact; not uncommonly indeed with the intention of support-ing some existing institution or interest by inventing for it an origin and an authority in the past which it could not truly claim. So, when the books of the Bible were examined freely like other literature and history and the different points of view of individual writings and the different accounts of the actual facts narrated and described were noted, the conviction grew that the Bible presented some at least of the characteristics of other ancient literature and history. For example, one result which was reached by all such students as we have in view was that our first three Gospels had all been composed at a considerable interval of time after the events which they narrated and gave us beliefs held in one or another little society of Christians at the time at which they were written, and included with their actual historical data a good deal of later reflexion and interpretation. Later experience had coloured the narrative of fact, and special aims and interests were reflected in some of the narratives when compared with others. This is true of the first three Gospels. It is still more conspicuous in the fourth, which is to be regarded as a theological treatise—an interpretation of the significance of Jesus in the scheme of things, suggested by the writer's own experience and the Logos-philosophy—rather than as a history of the details of His life and teaching while He was on earth.

So a new apologetic was required, and while many students were in search of some way of defending the Christian Religion without abandoning its traditional basis in history, the Abbé Loisy was one of the first to come forward with the theory that the Christian Faith was independent of any of the results of the historical and literary criticism of the Gospels. The faith of the Church—its whole doctrinal and institutional system—might be true, though the historical facts on which it had been believed to rest were other than had been supposed: although, that is to say, it can be traced as a gradual growth and developement from historical beginnings not ascertainable in detail as to the facts and our Lord's own consciousness and intentions in the way the Church has claimed. That is, no doubt, too rough a way of representing the thought and writing of so fine and delicate a mind as Loisy's. But let me take an instance or two. 'What think ye of Christ?' Every student of the history of doctrine knows that the formulation of the answer arrived at by the Councils of the fourth and fifth centuries, which represents the orthodox doctrine of the Church, was the outcome of many earlier attempts and discussions, the earliest of which are to be found in the New Testament itself, and that it states the Christian position in relation to various schemes of philosophy and ideas which were not in the minds of the writers of our Gospels. Yet the Church has always claimed for its formulation that it was true to the historical data furnished by the Gospels. In particular, it has assumed that the Gospels shew that our Lord in His lifetime thought of Himself as GOD, or indeed, as orthodox theologians have put it, 'as the Second Person of the Ever Blessed Trinity'. A Divine consciousness has been attributed to Him from the moment of His birth—as mediaeval painters depicted the Child in His Mother's arms with His three fingers raised in blessing while the adoring Magi bent low before Him.

Loisy is clear that all this is thoroughly unhistorical, and he will have nothing to do with the idea that some of the teaching of the grown man was of universal validity, and some only 'accommodated' to the times and the existing level of knowledge and, therefore, relative to it and of only temporary significance. For Loisy, the whole is relative to the historical environment of the era, and definitions and formulas can never have more than a provisional and relative value, as attempts to express the truth and to guide and stimulate faith in individual souls. How uncertain what are called the actual facts of the Gospel history are is shewn, for example, by the narratives of the Resurrection which indicate, he says, that the belief was a great act of faith rather than the result of what we might call the evidence of the senses.

I think we may fairly sum up Loisy's position on these questions by saying, though not in his own words, that the real facts were an undefinable sense of union with GOD on the side of Jesus and a belief that He was the Messiah who was to come, and a growing faith in Him, and in GOD as revealed in Him, on the side of His disciples. Or again we might say that the real facts were the religious experience of Jesus Himself and the religious experience of others of which He was at once the immediate cause and the centre. It is the substance of the Faith thus originated that matters, and the doctrinal system of the Church is of value as preserving and mediating and stimulating that Faith in all varieties of historical surroundings, so that its formulations must be elastic and adaptable to the ever-changing historical surroundings.

The historical surroundings of today are wholly different from those of the fifth century and its Christology. I need not remind you that in our doctrine of Christ we are stating a doctrine both of GOD and of Man. We interpret Christ according to the ideas we have of GOD and of Man, and our ideas today of GOD and of Man are very different from those of Christians of the fifth century. On this subject I find so admirable

13

a summary of part of one of Loisy's books in Archdeacon Lilley's review of modernism that I take a page
straight over (p. 74). It is the traditional Christology
of which he is speaking:

It was conceived in terms of a philosophy which no longer holds.
It depended on a view of GOD which conceived of Him as apart
from the world, on a view of the world which conceived of it as
apart from GOD. The traditional theory of the Incarnation was
framed to fit in with this conception of a transcendent GOD de-
siring to establish relations with a world which was separated
from Him. The Word was the intermediary of creation, an
emanation from GOD towards the world. Such theories have no
longer any meaning for us. The 'spatial transcendence' theory, as
Père Laberthonnière has aptly called it, must be abandoned because it no longer helps us to conceive of GOD. Every acquisition
of knowledge in our time forces us, if we would retain a vital
idea of GOD, to conceive of Him as immanent in the world and
in man, needing no intermediary in order to act upon and in both.
Physical science is forcing us to a fresh analysis of the religious
idea of creation, which will provide for GOD's immediate activity
in the world of nature. History is forcing us to a fresh analysis of
the idea of revelation which will provide for GOD's immediate
activity in the total spiritual developement of human society.
Psychology is forcing us to a fresh analysis of the idea of redemption
which will provide for GOD's moral action in the developement of
the individual soul. Out of this threefold analysis will issue a new
and fruitful realization of GOD as operant in the world and in man.
For the religious mind the rationalism which conceives of a purely
transcendent GOD and of a purely human Christ will become un-
meaning and impossible. The Christian faith that Christ is GOD
will be established through conceptions which the modern mind
can appreciate.

That seems to me to state the 'modernist' position
on the subject as well as it can be stated.

It is fundamentally conditioned by recognition of
the evolutionary process of the world and human
history and the conviction that GOD is 'in' the process,
in whatever way He may also be 'outside' it—local

and spatial metaphors being inevitable for us. There is no such chasm between GOD and Man as the traditional theology presupposes. Discovery by Man and revelation by GOD are different aspects of one continuous process.

But there is another factor in this modernist position which is not so clearly brought out.

Modernism implies no canonization of modern thought. It objects to the canonization of the thought of any particular epoch in the life of the race. It is this kind of canonization of the past that causes the very problem which modernism seeks to solve. And again, inasmuch as it holds that the doctrinal system of the Church is riddled through and through by the know-ledge that has accrued since it was built up, it might seem better to abandon it wholly and to seek to build up a new system on entirely different premisses. But modernism, as Father Tyrrell insisted, is quite as much interested in the past as in the present, in Tradi-tion as in modernity; and quite as much also in the future as in the present. So it seeks a new point of view, a new line of approach to the problem, so that nothing of permanent value in the old may be lost.

And yet again, just because it holds that the Christian revelation is not the revelation of a number of in-tellectual truths or propositions of a rational kind, but is the revelation of a way of life, an attitude to life and all its interests and activities, and therefore is social, it holds that this revelation is only to be understood and realized in a society with an ordered life of its own. And further, because it is convinced that in the historical society of the Church, whatever its formulas, there has always been true Christian experience; it cannot contemplate any severance from that stream of life. The synthesis it aims at must be effected in the Church itself.

3. The problem of Authority.

It is here peculiarly that the question of authority arises—the third of the problems. On this question Tyrrell was a chief exponent of modernist ideas. I should find it impossible to do justice to his thought in few words. What again and again he insists on is that the authority of the society must allow for the liberty of its members and must admit of the kind of growth and variety and newness that belong to life. It can never be stereotyped or absolute, or it sets itself in conflict with life and sterilizes it. There are no infallibilities.

I suppose that what was needed on behalf of the Roman modernists was that they should be allowed to continue their efforts to create within the Church itself a public opinion favourable to their new point of view without interference by the high officials of the Church. That was not to be. They were condemned and banished from the Church.

In England, in all the Churches, I suppose, there are some who would like to mete out the same measure to the exponents of new views. But the English tradition of liberty and freedom of discussion is too strong; the hold on Doctrine is too uncertain; the belief that Conduct is more important than Creed is too widespread; and, I must add, the 'established' Church of England, whose ideal of Catholicity has always implied the existence within it of different schools of thought, is too effective a bulwark against theological narrownesses for the policy of official suppression to prevail. Modernism, therefore, in all the chief characteristics I have named, remains in England within the Church as an active influence on it. It seems to me to offer the only possible basis for the synthesis of the old and the new world in things theological and religious; and at least in all Protestant Churches it is modernism that means union. It is hopeless to pursue union so long as our inherited systems of doctrine and institutions and organizations are regarded as anything but stages in an evolutionary process, in which the human factor is responsible for the means to the end, even if men in general have only a dim consciousness of either the process or the end and are dependent on the occasional prophet for direction and stimulus, and on the ever-present organizer and administrator for the readjustments which mark the different stages in the process.

In conclusion, how effectively modernism is at work in the world today is shewn by the widely-diffused alienation of men from all existing religious systems and the new interest in Religion itself, the recognition of it as in some way part of the very content of human life, and the serious endeavour to diagnose the phenomena of religious experience so as to find its essential character, as a symptom and an element of reality.

And again it is shewn by two reactions. On the one hand, we have the attempt to re-establish the authority of the Bible in the sense of the sixteenth-century

Reformers, or rather perhaps of their successors, with whom what was to the Reformers essentially the charter of the enfranchized soul became a binding code of unalterable laws[1]. On the other hand, among those who want a more living and present authority, there is the attempt to commend again the system and methods of the mediaeval Church as really meeting the religious ideas and needs of the world today.

It is often from the reactions to them that the tendency of new movements can best be judged. These two violent reactions help to shew what the way of modernism is.

[1] So Troeltsch somewhere.

§ II

THE USE OF HOLY SCRIPTURE TODAY[1]

The problem of the use of Holy Scripture today is part of a much larger problem, and I assume that when you invited me to read a paper to you on the subject, as a student to fellow-students and a priest of the Church of England to fellow-priests, you intended that I should at least try to put the problem in its setting, see it against its background, and get it in its right perspective.

It is sacred ground which we are to traverse and we need the guidance of the Spirit of Truth. But we have no right to expect the Truth to come to us without the labour and pains of making ourselves acquainted with all that is known as regards our particular subject. I agree with Lord Balfour that 'excesses of unbelief may be as extravagant as those of belief', but I am also sure that we are just as much responsible for our beliefs as we are for our unbeliefs. And that responsibility in its fullness is on those who have to teach and propagate their beliefs. What we clergymen believe and teach about the Bible today may determine whether it regains or not the place which it has had in the past, and has lost far and wide today—the place of the Great Book of Religion. Unless we can re-establish its value for the proper understanding of Religion, in the light of its history and in relation to all the new knowledge of our own time, it will cease

[1] A paper read to a Clerical Society in Surrey in 1925.

to have authority even in its rightful domain. But I suppose the question, What is its rightful domain? is the one we are met to discuss. And I take it that an introduction to our discussion should be general in character and that you do not wish me to practise any kind of economy of the truth as I see it.

Our difficulties are on us today, largely no doubt as a result of the unparalleled intellectual enterprise of the last fifty years or so, and the mass of new knowledge, new concepts and ideas, in all departments of human interest that it has accumulated. But in the particular subject we have in view they are also largely due to the economies practised by most English divines and scholars in the past as to the changes in point of view of the subject which the new knowledge entailed. These changes were not articulated in a way in which they could become familiar to the rank and file even of the educated classes.

Now, when we have all partly at least digested the new knowledge, we are in a state of discomfort or bewilderment. We are conscious everywhere in our religious system of incoherencies and incompatibilities. We can do some piecing and patchwork. Can we get a general point of view, a position, from which we can see the subject in relation to a whole?

I take it that you do not want me to go over the ground that has been debated for the last century and more and shew how studies in every department of ancient literature and history first, and then in all the departments we group together as the Natural Sciences, led—for all educated people who were not hypnotized by the idea that the inspiration of the

Bible implied the truth of everything in it—to the
position in which we find ourselves today, when for all
educated people, except the class which I have just very
roughly characterized, the evolutionary hypothesis is
at least dominant to the extent that any idea conflicting
with it is *ipso facto* discredited—not necessarily rejected, but bereft of the prestige of lineage which otherwise it might claim and enjoy. The prestige of the
Bible has suffered much weakening. We cannot use
it as it was used in the past. That, I assume, is the
position we are to face this afternoon, and we are to
recognize that it has come about in the course of the
ordinary progress of knowledge. We are to put ourselves on the highway of this course of human progress,
frankly and courageously, without any harking back
to the good old times and the happy days when people
could believe quite reasonably—because there was
nothing known to the contrary—many things which it
is just as unreasonable for us to believe today.

I take it again that our chief difficulty is due to the
fact that so many of the congregations with which we
have to deal are composed of people who must be
described as 'backward' in all these respects—at least
as facing backward rather than forward. I remember
well the kind of conspiracy of silence that characterized
many of my own honoured teachers; and, in general,
the clergy have been slow to assimilate the new knowledge and chary of indicating it to those whose religious ideas they could influence. Only a few months
ago Miss Maude Royden, at a gathering where many
clergymen were present, thought it worth while to
plead that they would cease using in their sermons

21

assumptions which they ignored or denied in conversation and in their published books.

I think the criticism was just, and I should carry it a stage further. I do not think that we are justified in using assumptions which we know are not supported by the general consensus of Christian students and scholars. It is not enough to be able to point to a few eminent upholders of a traditional opinion. We are all so slow after middle age to change our views.

It is no doubt because of this dead weight of conservatism that some of the reformers of all ages have been forced at times into what seems a kind of truculence. Some pulling down seems necessary in the process of repairs and building up again. And unless you make the background of your mind pretty clear, a congregation of Churchpeople will almost always assume that you believe what they were taught in their childhood and have heard ever since, and you will not be helping them to adjust their religious conceptions to their environment.

The temperament and mental outlook of the average religious man has been profoundly modified by the new knowledge. Even when he does not know exactly what it is, or what to think about it, he is conscious of it as a different atmosphere or environment. The old conception of a sacred literature was part of a conception of the world and man and GOD which only survives because it underlies the Christian Religion and the whole scheme of Christian Doctrine.

Let us first be clear on one fundamental point.

It has been said that 'No age has ever been so much interested in Religion as our own age' (we may ignore the cynical addition 'nor any so irreligious'). The question What is Religion? has been discussed with a fullness of knowledge of particular religions which was never available before, and we may remind ourselves how Schleiermacher insisted that it was only in particular positive religions that you could hope to find out the distinctive character of Religion. As a result, I do not think it can be denied that there is now general agreement that Religion belongs to the very content of human life. It is not something superadded from outside the universe, but in the universe there is something to which the religious emotion is our reaction. Among modern philosophers perhaps Prof. Alexander, himself a loyal member of the race with whose religious conceptions our own are most intimately connected, has given clearest expression to this conviction. This something is there, belongs to reality, and our capacity to respond to it shews that we are kin to it. It is in the universe and in us. It belongs to the ultimate nature of things—of the universe and of us. The religious emotion is unique.

It is not to be reduced to any of our primary instincts —self, sex, and herd—nor regarded as the highest sublimation of any one or of all of them, though it may make them all the channels of its activity. It cannot be explained adequately in terms of any of them.

I believe that the best-informed thought of today has reached this conclusion and that it is likely to become an axiom when the New Psychology, which has been extraordinarily informative in spite of all its absurdities, has settled down in its proper place among

23

the sciences. Obviously it is a conclusion of the highest importance—the matter of Religion is real.

In religious experience in all its forms, from the most rudimentary to the highest, man is in touch with reality. The religious consciousness is no will-o'-the-wisp, no phantom of a disorderly imagination. It points to, is a symptom of, or witness to, what in all the later stages of their evolution men have agreed in calling GOD. This religious consciousness is a factor of man's history and an integrating force in his life. It is through this that he attains a sense of moral values, and disorder ensues only from the survival of primitive conceptions side by side with the more developed and advanced.

It is to be trusted as a guide and a way to the truth of things: but its earlier manifestations and concepts and conclusions have no more value at a later stage as guides to truth than have the vestigial remains of our animal pedigree in our bodies value to enable us to fulfil our functions in life today.

What we could say of them is that they were relatively true. But what we mean by 'relatively true' is not easily understood; and if we say it we shall be regarded as shuffling. We must say plainly that they were not true as we know Truth today. Our standard of Truth must always be the highest and best that is known in our own time. It is instructive to learn something of the painful ways in which Truth is reached by man: but we lose the opportunity of some of the best moral lessons we need if we represent primitive ideas of GOD as tolerable for us today. They do survive in our sacred Scriptures and through them

24

in various ways in our Christian Religion—not nearly as clearly moralized and spiritualized in some of our doctrines and institutions as they should be. At least our handling of them in teaching the Bible should be sincere.

Again, there is, I think, general agreement that religious customs, rites, sacraments, acts and actions, precede any clear thought about them. There is only a dim sense of the sacred. Religious ideas or concepts, as such, come later, as attempts at explanation of an existing custom; and the first stage is myth-making. Such myth-making is the beginning of theology. Theology progresses with the upward progress of man in experience and knowledge of the world and its constituents—man's mastery of his environment and of himself—or whatever the process of man's developement from the lowest to the highest we know ought to be called. Theology is an intellectual output, just as worship and sacraments are the emotional output, of man. As these are the expression of his religious emotion, so theology is his attempt at rationalizing all his religious experience, or in other words building up a picture of the universe to satisfy the intellectual craving for explanation of experience. All such theologies are as truly pictures as were the myths of the first theologians, and they have been largely dependent on those myths. They have often used the same kind of imagery or symbol, reinterpreting it under the influence of a wider experience and knowledge of the facts of the world. The higher morality and the wider intellectual outlook of the later time has allegorized the cruder ideas of the past, and so been able as it were to come to terms with them, and maintain continuity of religious belief and association.

Where there is a sacred literature it embodies the early myths. Long habit of familiarity with them dulls the perception of their incongruity with later knowledge. They do not survive because they have what is called survival value, but because they are embedded in the 'sacred' tradition and institution and cult of the religious community. The folk-tales and myths and legends of the Hebrews are all incorporated in this way, and used, in much later books, in the collection of national literature of all kinds to which sacredness was attached.

This is what we have in our Old Testament: a good deal of folk-tale and myth and legend about the early history of the race and nation, many a *saga* of national heroes, a good deal of later history in a moralized form of a *tendenziös* character, much high political and religious thought, and real religious aspiration in prophecy and song and so on—all of it from the beginning to the end steeped in the consciousness of GOD and of His direction of human affairs with a purpose in view.

This great literature cannot stand for us today in the grand isolation from other contemporary religious literature which it once enjoyed for Christians. We know that it owes much to ideas derived from other peoples and their religious conceptions. It is not the only record of man's discoveries of GOD and GOD's revelations of Himself to man. But it is the only one in which the record can be traced through centuries of a people's life.

26

And it remains for us the classic expression of the history of man's gradual ascent in culture and civilization and of his knowledge of GOD growing with his growth of experience.

We must treat the Old Testament all through from this point of view as leading on to the New Testament and marking the stages by which man himself advanced in his adventurous voyage of discovery, shewing what he thought of GOD in his childhood and how his ideas became purified and enlarged as he grew; how, for example, he thought of GOD as writing laws on tables of stone before he came to know that they were only written on his heart, or thought of Him as doing and commanding things which at a later stage he came to know were wrong.

We are able to trace these processes in the history of Israel through the pages of the Bible. It is, as all are agreed, pre-eminently the book of religion, in which as nowhere else can be traced the course of the religious developements of a single race through different stages of its history: and primarily it is as such that we are bound to treat it. We are bound to treat the Old Testament as containing primitive myth and folk-lore and legend. Some of its 'history' is in the form of fairy-tales; all of it is like our stories with a moral. And we are bound to go further than this and point out the fact that the moral is often a low one.

It is demoralizing to teacher and to taught alike to adopt any other method of dealing with such stories, and intellectually it is disastrous.

It is almost inconceivable that Christians who accept the ethical teaching of Jesus as normative and

27

divine can ever have acquiesced in the eminently naturalistic ethic of some of the best known stories of the Old Testament. At least we cannot today, and the evolutionary background of modern thought makes it easy to insist on applying the New Testament standard to the less purified and moralized conceptions of humanity and GOD that abound in the Old Testament. To me it seems of paramount importance that they should be repudiated with the New Testament open in our hands. The fact that children in years or in mind rather revel in them makes the need for positive teaching about their real character all the more urgent even though there are moral truths of permanent value to be drawn from them.

At the time when the controversy roused by *Lux Mundi* was at its height, Archbishop Benson asked the question 'May not the Holy Spirit make use of myth and legend?' He had in mind some of the stories of the Old Testament only. But the thirty-five years which have run since then have gone far to do away with the idea that the mentality of the writers of the New Testament was essentially different from that of the writers of the Old Testament. We may hold that the New Testament contains much more of nearly contemporary and trustworthy history than the Old Testament, but I at least cannot doubt that it contains also legends and fairy-tales and a good deal of apparently straightforward narrative that describes, not things that actually happened as they happened, but rather what we are accustomed now to call the 're- ligious experience' whether of Jesus Himself or of some of those who were associated with Him.

About all such stories we ought to make it clear that they are like pictures of the symbolic kind—not the purely imaginative kind that aim at expressing only an idea of something that might be, but the kind that employ various forms of imagery to give to others a true impression of something actually felt or experienced. In such cases nowadays most of us would say I felt this or that, I thought this or that, the idea came to me, and so on. In the stories in the Gospels I have in view this kind of experience is narrated much more objectively. In some cases we can see the narrative grow in this kind of objectivity when we compare the earlier with the later versions.

It is the experience that is real. It is the same kind of experience that differentiates the religious from the rest. Many a Christian has had the assurance of the Fatherhood of GOD and of his own sonship. Most of them would not say that they had heard a voice saying 'Thou art my son', or seen a vision of the Spirit descending on them as a dove.

Let me take the instance of the story of the Temptation. Quite recently it was regarded as an account of a series of happenings on the plane of this earth, read as history at its face value. I suppose we all read it now as an allegorical or symbolic account of a mental or spiritual conflict through which our Lord passed before He entered on His public career, when different ideals and different methods of pursuing them were passed in review. Only He could know what happened in this 'valley of decision' in the desert. 'Vision' and 'voice' have often been the forms assumed by what we call religious experience, as they have been and still are of mania. It may well be the case that He regarded the 'temptation' to adopt the methods which He rejected as coming from the Devil, and that the whole experience was visualized by Him in the dramatic form in which it stands in our two Gospels. However that may be, unless the story is pure fiction, it must have come from Him in such a form. He must have told it to some of His disciples. And we must treat it as a parable in which we have expressed some of His fundamental convictions and the principles in accordance with which He intended to work for the ends He had in view.

The vision and the voice at the Baptism are again His alone. And the whole story of the Transfiguration has its origin in a psychic experience of which account is given in a similar symbolic and dramatic form.

This is the kind of history—the history of actual experience—which we have in our Gospels. It takes place in the desert, by the riverside, on the high mountain of the soul. It is some seventy years since C. H. Weisse—a pioneer in what may be called the attempt to apply the psychology of religious experience to the interpretation of the Gospels—declared that 'the high mountain [of the Transfiguration story] is not to be sought on the map of Palestine, but in the recesses of the spirit'.

I think we ought to let that principle be the basis of our teaching in regard to all such narratives. They do not tell us of phenomena that occurred for every one to see, but they do tell us the real experience of Jesus and some of His intimate friends.

Just as in regard to some of the stories of the Old

Testament we have to make the 'evolutionary' character of all that we call 'Revelation' plain before we can use them for any religious purpose today—or draw from them, as I said a moment ago, any moral truths; so in regard to many of the stories of the New Testament we have to take into account the mentality of the people from whom they come before we can draw from them the real character of the history which they narrate, and so their religious purport for us.

Let me try to put what I mean in relation to common Christian sentiment about the Bible.

It has always been felt that the real significance of the Bible was deeper and greater than anything in it that met the eye, that it contained riches of meaning beneath its surface that would abundantly reward those who worked deep down into its contents. Indeed, it has been urged that only they could reach its very truth. The superficial reader was in danger of missing the purport of some of its plainest statements.

So from the earliest days, at least from Tertullian's time in the second century, we find assertions that the Church alone was qualified to interpret the meaning of its Scriptures. Private judgement was ruled out of court. And the fear, widespread in later times, of putting the open Bible in the hands of the people without the teaching and guidance of ecclesiastical experts was not as unreasonable as it has been thought to be. The ordinary reader might easily misunderstand many things in the Bible.

It was this conviction that supported the allegorical and mystical interpretations by means of which piety

31

and religious imagination were fostered and fed, and spiritual intelligence and Religion quickened, even though it may be certain that no such meanings were in the writers' minds.

We have had a full dose of this method. I believe it is often now regarded as a dope, and in the way in which it has been applied I believe it has often been a dope. It was a real advance in both knowledge and Religion to insist on the primary historical reference and the literal meaning, and definitely to ban the old alchemy. And yet I believe that the old method may point us to what is the truth for us—the religious truth —of much in our Bible that stands as narrative of incident or fact. The writer recorded it as incident. Someone had made a story of it: but the fact itself was something of which the story was only a picture.

I know you will not all agree with me, but I am convinced that the fact behind such stories as the Feeding of the Multitude, the Turning of Water into Wine, the Raising of Lazarus, is the power that Jesus exercised over men's minds or souls. Whatever the author of the Fourth Gospel intended his readers to believe as to the physical facts, it is clear that he told his stories as illustrations of the truths of the spirit—truths of his own experiencing—which the discourses proclaim. In our modern phrase the 'values' which Jesus represented are man's sustenance, bread and wine, and his true life. To be united with His Spirit is to be in fellowship with the eternally true and real, it is to pass from death to life.

That Jesus was a great Faith-Healer is of course certain; but, in my judgement, all attempts to discriminate between the other narratives of so-called 'miracles' are as idle as are attempts to bolster them up by anything that modern science has revealed or is likely to reveal.

I am sure the time has come when they ought no more to be treated as true accounts of actual occurrences than we now treat the stories Jesus told to picture out His moral and spiritual teaching.

There are some it is true who can still derive trustworthy information about our future state and interests from the Parable of the Rich Man and Lazarus. And thirty years ago Dr Plummer could aver of the Parable of the Good Samaritan that Jesus was not likely to have invented such a story or told it if the incidents had not actually occurred. 'Moreover', he adds, 'the parable would have far more point if taken from real life'.[1] 'We may believe that the narrative is not fiction, but history'. Others have spoken of some of the narratives of the kind to which I am referring as 'acted parables'.

My own conviction is that the only history to which they bear witness is that of the impression produced by the personality and teaching of Jesus, and that this history of actual vital experience constitutes the permanent religious value of the narratives. I would use them, and have them used, for no other purpose. The old allegorical method of interpretation, which took them as symbolic of spiritual relations between the soul and GOD through its association with Jesus, arrived at the historical fact which is the truth of the narratives. I believe that frank teaching to this effect today

[1] *Gospel according to St Luke* Internat. Crit. Comm. pp. 285 f.

is the way to save them and their religious value for
the future, and for my own part I have found it both
intellectually and spiritually stimulating to those to
whom it has been presented, so far as I am able to
judge.

And now I turn to another of our difficulties today,
in some ways graver and more urgent than those that
arise from stories of happenings remote from common
experience.

I read somewhere lately of the widespread consciousness that the riddles of our modern and complex
world cannot be answered by texts from the Bible.
The meaning apparently was that it is useless to cite
sayings of Jesus such as those in the Sermon on the
Mount as having any authority in regard to the moral
and economic conditions of modern society. It is the
moral authority of Jesus that is questioned here. What
ought our attitude to be?

We are living in an age when authority of every
kind has to justify itself. We gladly remember, then,
that everyone who has ever attempted to expound the
Ethic of the Gospel has noted its inwardness and
spiritual freedom, its emphasis of motive and intention.
Its appeal is always to the individual conscience and
free will. It does not claim to impose itself. The only
authority it claims is that of its own intrinsic persua-
siveness. It is our own fault that Christ has been
presented to the world as a lawgiver, a legislator. And,
if He is to come to His own in these times, I think that
is the first point to which we should address ourselves.

I have constantly heard from the clergy in the
pulpit and elsewhere the phrase 'the law of Christ',

and I suppose I have used it myself. I never do now. For one thing, it is quite illogical to treat some of the sayings in the Sermon on the Mount as 'laws' to be enforced on human society, whether nominally Christian or not, and others as merely counsels of perfection for individuals. I need not specify instances.

I am sure we ought to drop the misleading use of the word 'law'. All the sayings represent ideals. Some of them may seem to be irreconcilable. If we recognize Jesus as supreme in the realm of ends—of spiritual values—none the less it is clear that He left to us the responsibility of deciding the measure in which in any given set of circumstances in our always-changing personal and social and economic conditions we could approximate—in the ordering of our own lives and the lives of others that we could control—to realization of His ideals. (Parenthetically let me say I have no doubt that a second marriage is as inconsistent with the ideals of Jesus as is lending money on interest, or refusing to give to everyone that asketh you.) He never envisaged a human society such as ours, and while all our experience is leading us to the conclusion that a society based on some of His cardinal convictions is the only hope of our present civilization, yet we know that it cannot be one in which all His sayings are 'laws'.

It is morally confusing to have some sayings of Jesus treated as laws imperative on Christians, and others, on the same plane of ethical outlook and conduct, as negligible. It is surely better to let all stand alike and make their own appeal to the individual conscience and imagination as the ideals of the Great Teacher;

3-2

and especially with those whose ethical position is in the making, or unsettled by new ideas and needing to be remade, sayings of Jesus will not carry authority unless it can be shewn that they are applicable to the facts of life in the world as it is. Authority has to justify itself, and when it is claimed for rules of life which experience does not confirm—and the experts in the particular subject reject—its impressiveness vanishes.

We have lost balance and proportion; or rather we have not yet acquired it, for the Church began law-making at once. In the sphere of Christian Ethics this balance and proportion is being forced on us today, and we can only make the ethical teaching of the New Testament our standard by subjecting it to what Dr Westcott used to call 'a proportionate interpretation'.

Our business is to point to the ideals, and in the fulfilment of them sometimes to run directly counter to their literal sense.

Examples will suggest themselves at once to us all. Are you to 'give to everyone that asketh you'? No, but pay your poor rates willingly; don't try to cut down wages to a minimum; and give all the help you can to individuals you know who are out of work because there isn't work for them to do. Are you to 'lend freely expecting nothing back'? Certainly not; but be content with moderate profits or interest on your money; let interest on loans be regulated in pro- portion to the risk of loss, and give out and out as fully as you will. And what of divorce or remarriage? Of course they are dead against the ideals of Jesus, but

36

marriage was not one of His own experiences. Face the facts, all the facts of human nature and life in the world as it is, and beware lest the light that is in you be darkness.

Do not let us talk of the 'law' of Christ, as if we had from Him anything that we could take straight over into what we know as legislation. If we insist instead on His moral insight, His attitude to life, His ideals; His revelation to men of their best selves and His call to them to respond; then we need not fear that He will not have the kind of authority which was all that He desired. The Gospel ethic treats men as free moral personalities, and critical appreciation must precede vital appropriation. Only then does it really become true for us.

If we turn for a moment to more narrowly theological questions, our traditional theological system has been shattered. It is from the Bible that we have to build it up again, no doubt, but with Evolution as our guide and the picture-book conception of the Bible always in our minds.

To take St Paul as chief example of the theologian, we have to exercise the same critical appreciation with regard to his theology, and always we have to remember that theology and anthropology go hand in hand, and much of St Paul's anthropology was wrong. There wasn't a Fall as he supposed, Death isn't a result of Sin but part of the process of the world, the Potter image is immoral. These factors of his theology and some of his more speculative pronouncements about the future can have no authority for us. They are merely vestigial survivals of his pre-Christian

37

inheritance and not supported by anything in the teaching of our Lord.

My paper has been too long already. As I read it over I feel that I have not avoided what I wished to avoid, namely, 'bringing coals to Newcastle'. There may be some fuel in it fit for lighting our discussion. Or if you will, I shall be well content that you should let our discussion run on altogether other lines. Only I beg leave to say that I did not think it was worth while that we should spend our time on any kind of appreciation of what is called the devotional value of the Bible, about which it may be assumed that we are all agreed. We know that one who knows his Bible can always turn to passages in it that meet his needs. New meaning, new force, is found in them, because he is passing through the same moral and spiritual experiences as those out of the fullness of which the men who wrote them spoke. Unregarded once, or only faint and fugitive in the impression they made, they become to him very words of GOD addressed to him alone—to warn or to enlighten, to steady and guide, to strengthen or comfort him, through the temptations and problems, the joys and the desolating sorrows of his life. That is the region of the Bible's true inspiration.

But just in conclusion I cannot avoid the trite remark that human nature changes very slowly. It has taken at least half a million years to bring Man to his present state from the moment when, in the cosmic process which had then been working many millions of years, he first emerged. He hasn't yet had more than a few thousand years of civilized life. Some of our most convinced evolutionists and learned biologists are interpreting the facts they find as revealing an inherent urge towards higher forms of life; and some of them speak of this general characteristic as the tendency of the whole universe to Deity. They do not of course use, or as scientific investigators allow, the personal terms in which our essentially human 'religious emotion' expresses itself. That would be to go beyond their province. But to many of us it must seem that our religious picture of GOD and His age-long purpose—as a picture in personal terms—gets support today which a purely mechanistic description of life refuses it. And so the Bible, which is permeated with the sense of the purpose and will of GOD, and even represents that purpose as having had already once its proleptic realization in the Person of our Lord, must stand side by side with the latest book on Evolution for those who really want to know the scientific truth of things.

FACTS OR VALUES[1]

καὶ πᾶς ὁ λαὸς ἑώρα τὴν φωνήν. 'And all the people saw the voice'.
Exodus xx. [xxi.] 18.[2]

So the experience known as the giving of the Law on Sinai is described in the Greek version which was the only form of the Old Testament known to the early Christians.

I suppose to the ordinary reader the phrase would seem nonsense, and the textual critic would be busy at once on his task of emendation, either of verb or of noun, according as palaeographical probability could be the more plausibly invoked: yet Philo,[3] commenting on the passage, says it is the right way to describe Divine revelations which men seem to see rather than to hear. 'All that GOD says, they are not words but deeds, and the eyes give judgement on them before the ears.' That is to say, religious experience is not really mediated either by the eyes or by the ears: but in the description of it all the senses may be requisitioned, and an experience of the soul, of the personality, will be stated as one in which the senses all played a part—and yet not each its appropriate part, but seeing was hearing and hearing was seeing.

We are all familiar with the phenomena of dreams,

[1] A Sermon preached in St Sepulchre's, Holborn, at the Annual Eucharist of the Churchmen's Union, 1920.

[2] Cf. also Revelation i. 12, 'And I turned to see the voice which spake with me'.

[3] de Decalogo 11.

in which every detail of a scene—a drama, a tragedy, a jest or a terror, with act and sound—is vividly present to every sense. So the idealist painter 'sees' his picture in his mind before he gets it on his canvas: and the musician 'hears' his music as he writes it down, or the melody runs in his head for weeks before: and again, as he reads the script, he hears.

What is language to do with experiences like these? What are the facts? How are we to state them?

One of the younger Oxford philosophers, Mr Harley Walker, has lately published a little book on *The Construction of the World in terms of Fact and Value*,[1] which contains the results of acute thinking expressed with a lucidity rarely attained by writers on such subjects. It is a subject of primary importance for Christian theology and ethics today, and those of us who, like myself, are not philosophers, must be grateful for a treatment of the subject that we can fairly well understand.

We doubt a great many of what are commonly called the 'historical facts' on which the Christian Religion is based. I wish that everyone, including all the distinguished company that is to be assembled at Lambeth next month, might be required to pass an examination in this little book before he dared to affirm for himself, or to require from anyone else, belief in 'the historical facts stated in the Creeds'. We need to make clearer to our own minds what are the 'facts' on which our religion depends; and though there are other questions of practical urgency which

[1] *The Construction of the World in terms of Fact and Value*, by C. T. H. Walker (B. H. Blackwell, Oxford).

are to engage your attention today, I venture to suggest this as one that calls for present consideration. We cannot allow ourselves—we cannot allow the great cause of the Christian Religion—to be tied down to popular views of fact and fiction, of fact as something which happens rather than of something which is, or of truth and value as though the one could be ultimately independent of the other. To identify the Christian Faith with belief in all the 'facts' recorded in the Gospels or the Creeds was possible so long as no historical or literary criticism of our documents was allowed. It is absurd today. We have to search deeper to find the real historical foundation of our Faith, and we can only continue the use of our ancient Creeds and formularies because we believe that the really religious convictions they embody are the same as our own. Yet I venture to think that the time has come when such an association as The Churchmen's Union might take action to amend further the terms of the subscription which the clergy make, and in particular to bring to an end the 'articling' which pursues them all their lives, and put the emphasis on the living contents of Faith rather than on beliefs as to facts in the past.

Mr Harley Walker is at pains to accentuate the distinction between fact and value, and to note that Science is concerned only with facts and the connexion of one fact with another, and is entirely neutral as to values; while at the same time he insists that reality is only found when fact and value are combined.

It is of course on such a combination that the truth of Religion depends. It is in its essence indifferent to the *data* of Science and of History—the things 'given', of which there may be knowledge; for it is clear that the thing that happens, which Science can observe and History record, always eludes complete definition. There is constantly a clash of values, and it is only a true estimate of values that can give us the fact in its fullness.

In contrast with Science, Religion is concerned with the estimate of value, because it is concerned with personal experience, personal apprehension of what the subject of experience feels to come to him from outside himself, to be given to him, by a bombardment of impressions in which seeing is hearing and hearing is seeing. Whatever the 'fact' may be, it is its bearings on himself personally that he can appreciate. He can always be much more sure what the fact means to him, what the action of it on him is, and what his own reaction to it is, than he can be as to what the fact itself is. This is indeed the fact to him.

Let me take a 'historical' instance, in the record of which there seems to be a clash both of fact and of value.

There is a crowd gathered round a speaker, whom some of them regard with indifference or idle curiosity and others believe to be a great prophet. At a moment when feeling is tense on the part of some of them and the speaker himself is profoundly moved, discerning the hour as critical, his conception of his mission and whole career at stake, and pours out his soul in an earnest appeal to GOD to vindicate Himself in the words, 'Father, glorify thy Name':—something happens. The whole atmosphere was, as we say, electrical. There was a burst of pent-up emotions.

43

Some said there was a sound of thunder; others that an angel spoke to him. To the speaker there came the assurance that he craved for—he heard the words, 'I have glorified it and I will glorify it again'. What, then, was it that happened? What, here, is the historical fact? We have three descriptions of it: which is right? Or were there at the same moment three different but coincident facts? There were three different experiences: if we are to say that there was only one fact, it is certain that in this case fact and value were disparate.

There was some kind of stimulus, and in the group it produced three different reactions. The different mentalities reacted to it in different ways, by that selective process by which we become aware of our environment in proportion to the range of our consciousness. It is in assigning to a fact its just value that we arrive at the truth about the fact: not in our description of it as a fact. In this case the speaker who heard definite words and the bystanders who said an angel had spoken to him were substantially at one in their valuation. Encouragement came to him from a source that both alike regarded as transcendental. If they were right, then for them fact and value were combined: unity was achieved, they were in touch with reality. GOD had ranged Himself on the side of Jesus—He had affirmed 'the conception of an hour'.

The other bystanders did not understand what was happening. Whatever it was, it only reached their outer senses—they said it thundered: for them nothing out of the way had happened. Some of them probably did not hear the thunder:—nothing had happened. Only, the speaker recovered himself and went on with his discourse with a new note of confidence.

We cannot get nearer to the actual fact than this.

And if the narrative be regarded not as a historical account of any actual incident, but rather as an imaginative construction of experience, in the form of an impressionist picture, with no one definite recorded or remembered fact as its substance: yet it is surely *ben trovato*—the design is well conceived, well carried out. There are *data* enough recorded in the other Gospels to shew that this was the kind of thing that was constantly happening in the career of Jesus as regards Himself and others alike—the Baptism, the Temptation, the Transfiguration, Gethsemane. He was the subject of remarkable experience Himself and the medium of remarkable experience to others. For them He was a true creator of experience. Things were constantly happening. What were the facts? Some of them He himself described—the Temptation, for example. There was a time, measured by years a very short time ago, when the description He gave of it was generally believed to be a literal transcript of three successive incidents—an account of three scenes in an enacted drama. The latest exposition of the Temptation, just published by the S.P.C.K., seems loth to abandon this view of the facts. But those are not the facts that the story discloses to us today, though it is possible that the experience was not only told by Him in that dramatic form, but actually present to His consciousness at the time in the form in which He told it; as the visions of the prophets and mystics of all ages

45

are seen by them and the voice of the Lord—or it may be the Devil—is heard; and they tell of a real experience that has 'come' to them—not one that has been invented; and they give to others what first was 'given' to them. In the story of the Temptation the actual fact was not what the story states. No Devil came and took Him up into the holy city and set Him on a pinnacle of the temple. That is only one of many possible descriptions of the actual experience. The real fact was the experience itself—the fact that Jesus felt the pull of one possible policy and definitely faced it and turned His back on it. The fact is to be found in His valuation of two conflicting ideals and His resolute choice between them. That is the fact—the determination of His line of action.

And so, all through the story of His life, of scientific definition of incident after incident we have none. Of poetic or dramatic description narrative after narrative is full; and even if every narrative implies and reflects the actual happenings, it is the valuation of them that determines the account.

Such stories as those of the Nativity and the Resurrection-appearances can only be regarded as records of fact in the same way as the story of the Temptation or of the Voice from heaven. The narratives must all be interpreted in relation to each other.

The only fact that we can certainly recover is the fact of the experience—the impression that remained, the valuation of it whether by Jesus Himself or by those who told the story. If I may venture slightly to emend Bede's definition of 'the true law of history', I would suggest that it is the single-minded transmission, not so much of current belief as of the impression which events produced, as exactly as the historian can on the one hand perceive and retain or recover it, and on the other hand convey it. The perception itself involves valuation, so far as it is not merely a sense impression, and the expression of it and the transmission of it to others, if it is not instantaneous, is liable to a further process of valuation into which a still larger subjective element enters.

'Nothing shall prove twice what once was proved'; but the record of what was believed to be a Revelation of Reality serves its purpose, and proves again and again what it was to prove, if it conveys to later generations the same estimate of values and rouses in them the same convictions, the same faith as regards GOD and Man and the meaning and purpose of life, as the original experience created. Its definitions or descriptions of events will of necessity be entirely subject to the Science or to the tastes and fashions, literary and historical, of the time of its origin. They can never be verified in detail.

But the Revelation, *ex hypothesi*, is a psychic process —the disclosure of reality to persons. Its content can be verified in individual experience, so far as verification in the things of the spirit can be attained. It produces conviction, an assurance of the reality of the values of life it creates.

Only life itself can furnish verification of a theory of life. The process of the great drama of 'redemption' is eternally the same. Once achieved, the way to the goal is open. Individual after individual may freely pass along it. But he must go through the same

47

experience in his own person. He must become the *persona* of the drama. He must live the part.

The Christian Religion may be true or false; but its truth or its falsity does not depend on the accuracy of any one narrative in the Gospels, and therefore not of all of them taken together, but on the truth or untruth of the total experience of Christians. Is the GOD-theory true? Is it the purpose and character of GOD that is revealed to us in Jesus? Is it, or is it not, the mind of Christ that must be in us if individually we are to become the persons we are meant to be, and the world and the race of mankind, human society as a whole, is to fulfil its end?

Is this Christian experience, age after age renewed, re-enacted—not the abnormal experience of 'the Saints' but the average Christian experience—a mere *mirage*, an unsubstantial creation of men's hopes and fears and emotions? or is it ours only because it is based on an ultimate truth and reality to which our own existence belongs—of which it is in part the expression? When 'all the people saw the voice'; when the Word of the Lord came to the prophets; when Jesus saw the heavens opened and heard the voice 'Thou art my beloved Son'; when a few of the disciples saw and heard their Friend and Master after His death at their evening meal; when He comes to two or three of us as we walk and talk and maybe are sad; when we represent and re-enact (as we are doing now) the eternal drama of man's salvation through service that is sacrifice of self, and renew our allegiance to the ideals of life He taught us, and receive the broken bread and poured-out wine, and seek to identify our-

selves with the actual experience, the process of redemption, through which He passed, and become in
purpose and intention for the moment one with Him
—so that the sacrament is to us efficacious—our
dramatization of the mystery brings to consciousness
that which it depicts:—are these experiences illusory?
or are they indeed the reflexion in a moment of time
of an eternal abiding reality?

It is by the valuation we put upon this great
historical experience that our faith as Christians must
be measured.

We do indeed depend on history. For justification
of our faith we appeal to it. We affirm that once in the
long history of the world the process of 'salvation' was
really achieved by one who was born a man and lived
as man and was put to death and shewed Himself
living after His death to those that had eyes to see and
ears to hear what His spirit said to them, and that in
the same spirit He has shewn Himself and spoken to
every generation since. And we affirm that in every
generation those who have made His values of life
their own have reached the 'salvation' He achieved.

It is faith in His GOD and His values of human
personality and life that is the heart of the Creed of
a Christian, and if the Church is to win the best men
and women and reclaim the worst it must make it
clear that this alone is the faith it demands of all its
members alike.

EVOLUTION AND CHRISTIAN THEOLOGY[1]

We have to consider this afternoon two of the greatest Revelations that have ever come to man—revelations of truth about himself and the world to which he belongs, separated from each other in what we know as time by nearly two millenniums.

The first was made long ago in the strange experience, in many ways still as elusive as ever, of which the Christian Religion was the outcome, with its organization of cult and institutions.

The second has come to us in the lifetime of all the older ones of us who are present here, and much of it in the last twenty years. It is the experience of all the new knowledge, in all the departments of human interest and activity in which scientific investigation is possible: literary, historical, physical, chemical, biological—what not? This experience has given us a new view of the World and Man.

In each case there was a central figure, an outstanding personality, in whom and with whom the new experience began. It is his experience first— the revelation came to him first. But he was not isolated or alone. There was a public ready to appreciate the experience, enter into it, make it their own. Otherwise it never would have been a revelation. Man, groups of men, mankind on a large scale have to attest a revelation. Is it truth or not? Only Man can decide.

This kind of attestation has been given abundantly

[1] The Jowett Lecture delivered in the Mary Ward Settlement Hall on Tuesday, 22 February, 1927.

to the revelation of which Jesus of Nazareth was the subject and, regarded as the Christ, also the centre. In consequence of it men gave a new account of themselves and the world. In our fashionable phrase a new valuation of human life ensued.

The same kind of attestation is being given now to the revelation made in our own days. All the new knowledge has resulted in a new view of the significance of the universe and of man's place in the whole scheme of things. There is an evolutionist temper and an evolutionist attitude to life widespread and spreading among those who couldn't give a very lucid account of Evolution. And that is the conclusive test of the victory of an idea—not whether it has convinced the *intelligenzia*, but whether it has so passed into the common consciousness of men that they do not know that they are influenced by it.

The Christian revelation triumphed in this way in the past, the Evolutionist revelation is triumphing in this way now. At present the victory is more visible outside the Churches than within them. The Churches are confused because the world at large has learnt a truth which they have not yet assimilated.

Anyone who wants at this moment to be able to give a true account of himself—to place himself in the whole scheme of things—should be familiar not only with the Bible but also with one of the latest volumes on Evolution such as the one that was published in the summer of 1925 with Dr Wilson's fine essay on the religious effects of the new knowledge[1].

[1] *Evolution in the light of modern knowledge*: a collective work (Blackie and Son, 1925).

But the Christian revelation of which I have been speaking is not identical with Christian Theology, and the subject on which I was invited to speak today is the relation of Evolution to Christian Theology.

Both terms 'Evolution' and 'Christian Theology' are used so loosely that anyone speaking of either of them must begin by trying to define the sense in which he uses them.

There is a technical sense of the term 'Christian Theology'.

In that sense it embraces the decisions of General Councils of the Church and the Creeds and definitions of a doctrinal kind which those General Councils drew up or sanctioned. That is an ascertainable *corpus* of Christian Doctrine. And the teaching of the Fathers and Great Doctors of the past, so far as it was not inconsistent with those decisions, has usually been taken as a kind of interpretative commentary or supplement to be referred to in case of ambiguities. There you have 'Christian Theology' called by its professors 'orthodoxy'—right opinion or belief. The definitions are usually crisp and clear enough, though to understand what they meant at the time you must know the background of thought and idea and all the circumstances in which they were drawn up.

But there is also a wider sense of the term. We all know that the epithet 'Christian' is one of the most ambiguous that are in use, and those of us who are members of the Church of England as established by law are encouraged to claim a good deal of freedom in our judgement as to what is 'Christian Theology'. The Elizabethan Act of Supremacy of 1559 does indeed set up as a criterion the doctrinal decisions of the first four General Councils and any other that rested on the express and plain words of Scripture. But almost all that our Articles of Religion have to say about General Councils is that they 'may err, and sometimes have erred, even in things pertaining unto God' (Art. xxi).

Since that time, at every turning point in the history of the Church of England, interpretation has grown more and more free from technical limitations. Interesting illustrations of this fact were given a few years ago in a little book called *Conscience, Creeds, and Critics* [1] by Mr C. W. Emmet, one of the ablest theological scholars of his generation. And more recently still a bishop of Oxford refused to regard as 'unorthodox' teaching about the Resurrection that was the direct negation of the belief on the subject which for centuries all bishops at their consecration had to profess.[2]

It would be easy to cite doctrines which have been generally held by those who profess and call themselves Christians, and have been supported by the full weight of ecclesiastical authority for ages, which I suppose nearly everyone present here today would say were not 'Christian' at all. I have no doubt that many of us in turn are holding on to doctrines in the belief that they are Christian on which our Christian successors of a later time will pass a similar judgement. For I do not doubt that the Christian Religion in the future will succeed in adapting itself to new knowledge, new

[1] Macmillan, 1918.
[2] See H. D. A. Major *A resurrection of relics* preface p. x (Blackwell, 1922).

53

ideas, new conditions of life and thought, as it has done in the past; and in spite of some reactionary tendencies at the moment I anticipate an evolutionary transformation of its Theology in the near future, factors of it which at present are dormant becoming dominant. For it is my conviction, as I shall indicate further, that we have never yet had a really Christian system of Theology. The system we know was about 500 years in the making. It is scarcely half that time since some of the chief facts and ideas which are the furniture of all our minds today began to be known and held; and it is only during a tenth of that time— some fifty years—that the evolutionist hypothesis and the discoveries of modern science, and the new methods and new knowledge of every kind, have effected those changes in our outlook on the world, and human life and history in it, that have made all views that do not take them into account seem out of focus—not really having to do with the world we know.

The Theology which has been deemed Christian in the past, of course, from the very conditions under which it came into being, does not take account of them.

But, as we have seen, a Theology may be held to be Christian which in parts at least runs counter to what had previously been regarded as Christian. We want a definition of the term, but how are we to get it?

We cannot make it depend on the teaching of Jesus for at least three sufficient reasons: one, that we cannot always determine precisely what that teaching was from the accounts of it that have come to us; another, that His teaching was conditioned by the ideas about the world and GOD's relation to it and ways of acting in or on it that belonged to the common notions of His age; and a third, that all that is specifically Christian depends on an interpretation of His own place in the whole scheme of things, which was hardly even implicit in His actual teaching, was only arrived at as a result of experience after His death, and was really a valuation of His significance in the light of His whole life and its impact on the world. So we could not make the teaching of Jesus the criterion of a Christian Theology.

We must have included in our criterion the valuation of Him of which the doctrine of the Incarnation became the generally accepted expression.

There may be found some day a better way of expressing it in relation to current ideas and thought —a better category than 'incarnation', though the history of language in general and theological terms in particular rather suggests that we are likely to keep the term and enlarge its meaning. But the valuation of the fact of Jesus and the experience associated with Him which it represents must, it seems, determine the sense of the word 'Christian'.

So all that I should like to commit myself to in the way of definition is the negative opinion that no Theology can be called Christian that is inconsistent with the fundamental idea of the doctrine of the Incarnation.

This idea must be central in a 'Christian' Theology: it must inspire it and permeate it—be the heart and life of it.

I should expect general agreement with that proposition—but a good deal of difference of opinion as to what 'the fundamental idea of the doctrine of the Incarnation' is. Jesus is recorded to have once asked His disciples, 'Who say ye that I am?'—He asked them to try to place Him in their scheme of things. And before the large world view of 'Incarnation' was suggested, they gave mere bits of answers with all the marks of time and place and personal limitations on them. Peter made the first, a paradoxical answer for a Jew—'Thou art the Christ'; and that idea was afterwards filled out and transfigured by the rich experience and imagination of St Paul so that the term could outgrow its Jewish associations and bear meanings which no one before had connected with it. And various other answers were given from different points of view, representing what individuals or groups had found in Him, like 'Lord' and 'Saviour'. And we have descriptions such as 'GOD in Christ reconciling the world to himself', or 'He that hath seen [Jesus] hath seen the Father' and 'He and the Father are one'—descriptions which are equivalent to partial answers to the question. Or folk-tale and legend—'myth' in the Platonic sense of the word— were invoked to help the answer out, like the stories of the Nativity and the Visit of the Magi.

All of these perhaps contribute something to the idea of the Incarnation. Certainly they have all influenced the traditional doctrine.

But I think we can afford to leave them on one side and go back to the fountain head of the idea, and I should not find that in St Paul's phrase in Col. ii. 9 'in him [Christ] dwelleth all the fulness of the Godhead

bodily', but rather in St John's 'the Logos became
flesh'. And of course not in that phrase isolated by
itself, but in its context. It is a whole philosophy of
existence that is implied in the prologue to the Fourth
Gospel, and when we give to the question 'Who say
ye that I am?' the answer 'the Logos become flesh',
we are saying quite as much about the world and ourselves as we are saying about Him. It is part of a great
complex of ideas.

What is this complex? Well, the learned and studious
scholars, the antiquarians of our religion (I refer to
them with the respect which is born of some knowledge
of their work), have long been busy with the question
of the origins of the Johannine conception. Where
did the writer get it from? The Old Testament *Memra*?
or Philo's Logos? or the Stoics? Or was it an idea in
the air, like Evolution today, that he caught up and
used? We are not concerned now with this question,
how he got it, but only with the question what it was,
what use he made of it. It is certainly a great idea
that he is handling. The term was there, ready to be
used, and it was a term that meant both 'thought'
and 'word', inward functioning and outward expression—thinking, reasoning, planning, and the
outcome of all these.

But he was a thinker who was not fettered by
technical terms. Besides the great word GOD, with
which no religious thinker can dispense, he used only the
terms of ordinary experience, like this term Logos, and
life, and light, terms which will never grow obsolete as
long as the world and Man exist: and his doctrine of
the Incarnation was stated by him very simply.

To find a place for Jesus in the whole scheme of things, he went back to the beginning and thought of the world we know as having its origin in a plan or purpose of which the existing order is the outcome. It is of course GOD's plan and purpose, and GOD's inward functioning and outward expression. It is a thoroughly organic conception.

The plan and purpose had never been realized fully. There was order in the world. In the Greek in which this thinker thought there is only one word for 'order' and 'world'. There could be no world without order. But it was not ordered yet as it was meant to be. It is an ordering process that has been going on from the beginning. For this thinker there is nothing haphazard about it—no blind chance, no fortuitous concourse of atoms, to make the world of Nature and of Man. All things come into being in accordance with purpose, and apart from that purpose was not anything made that has been made. It is the purpose that gives life to the whole, and is the light in what else would be darkness.

It is clear that this thinker is affected by the picture-story of the beginning of things with which our Bible opens, and he thinks of Man in particular as the highest outcome or exhibit of the ordering process. There has been darkness, and darkness still broods among men wherever this purpose-light of the scheme is not discerned, and their life is not true life unless it is directed to the furthering of the ordering process of the design: knowing the design and helping to fashion things after it.

Every man that is born into the world has within

him as his own a germ of the life and a glimmering of the light. He has the potency of becoming, in the Hebrew idiom, a 'child' or 'a son' of the true Life, a son of Light;—or when the personal form is used, instead of the abstract, a son of GOD.

In some of them the germ didn't grow as they grew, the light didn't lead them. But others became conscious of the purpose and followed the light and lived the life. These were all those whom Justin Martyr, a later writer of this school of thought, called 'the Christians before Christ'. But to our interpreter of history, whom we know as St John, there is no 'before Christ' in this sense of the term—nor was there really to Justin.

For the design for Man is in the beginning, and all the time, and all through the stages of the process. It is something trying to find expression, trying to realize itself, to shape Man to its form and likeness, patient but persistent[1]. It isn't anything imported into the world from outside; there never was a world without it. It is at the heart of the universe, the secret of its process, and its goal. Just in so far as it emerges or is manifested there is light and life.

And St John's valuation of Jesus is just that in Him this purpose for all men did emerge in fullness in His own consciousness, was visibly realized or, as He says, embodied, and made manifest to men in His life. The ideal was seen, full of grace and truth, in all its attractiveness and power of revealing their real selves to men, in a human life which in its quality and achievement reached the highest level.

[1] It is the 'formula' for Man, if I may borrow from Mr E. Bevan (*Later Greek Religion* Introd. p. xv).

That is the Christian doctrine of the Incarnation at its fountain head, as St John sets it out. And my thesis is a very simple one. Positively, it is that a really Christian Theology should be permeated through and through by the conception of the world and Man to which the phrase 'the Logos became flesh' belongs. If this conviction about the significance of Jesus in the whole world process controls it through and through, it is a Christian Theology. And negatively, my thesis is that doctrines which do not cohere with this conception, or are drawn from tales or pictures that are not like the truth it represents, are not really Christian and may be—and ought to be—eliminated from a Theology that claims to be Christian, whatever learned authority or popular prestige they enjoy.

If these two propositions are accepted—and I think that on their merits they must be accepted—then the new revelation of knowledge, of which 'Evolution' is the label, that has come to our generation is not out of harmony with the fundamental idea of Christian Theology. For 'Evolution' presents a world view closely similar to the Johannine, and its findings about the world and man's history in it are such as admit of the religious interpretation which the Logos doctrine offers.

And on the other hand, those elements in the traditional Theology, with which the facts revealed by Evolution clash, are found, on reconsideration of them, to be either survivals of primitive or pre-Christian religious ideas or philosophical pre-suppositions, which were never more than superficially Christianized, or else parasitical growths that are symptoms of disease.

I think that to all of these today the line of the old Greek tragedian may be applied—

οὐ πρὸς ἰατροῦ σοφοῦ
θρηνεῖν ἐπῳδὰς πρὸς τομῶντι πήματι.

In other words, the time for smooth words about them has passed. It is time to cut them out of our Theology.

Among these we must surely place the idea that the Divine operation in the world is especially revealed to men in unusual events and acts, with disturbance of the natural order, as it is known in general experience, and what we commonly call 'miraculous' apparatus.

Jesus Himself, though He believed that all things were possible to GOD, refused the signs that popular opinion looked for from the prophet and deliberately put aside as a suggestion of the Devil the idea that He might depend on 'miracle' for success in His mission. Yet His history has come down to us with all the accompaniments that were expected to attest theophanies, and our traditional theology has presupposed this idea of Divine Revelation and operation, and contrasted it with the prosaic mode of man's discovery by his own unaided efforts.

Again, the theory of Man's original state as one of bliss from which he fell by some fault of his own was widely current as an explanation of his sense of dissatisfaction with himself and his environment, his capacity for better things and his weakness to achieve them.

The doctrine of 'original sin' which presupposes such a theory of original righteousness was no part of the earliest Christian teaching, and in the fifth century Augustine, its chief exponent, found his strongest support for it in a mistranslation of St Paul on the one hand and on the other hand in the existing practice of baptizing infants. [Baptism was held to convey forgiveness of sins, and why should infants be baptised except that they were already at birth in a state of sin?] But it has permeated the teaching of the Church with false views of Man's history and of human nature, and the process of restoration which it suggests is recognized today as arbitrary and unethical. Here if anywhere in our traditional Theology the clean slate which the evolutionary sponge provides will be all gain.

For in these matters today we are not left to mere guesswork. We know enough about Man's history to be able to say that it has been from the beginning a splendid struggle against almost overwhelming odds. Whatever plan there is, it has been part of it that Man should fight his own way to higher stages of being and life. Wherever the power to do this comes from, he has had to use it as his own, as much a part of himself as those factors of his being that tend to keep him back or pull him down.

We rejoice that we can see Evolution as a creative process; but as regards the evolution of Man the creature has himself a very large part to play in the creation.

I anticipate nothing but good, and a great stimulus to further progress of mankind, from the fullest use in our Theology of the real facts as we know them.

The question of course arises whether such beliefs of the past and the stories in which they are embodied have not still some place in the realm of Truth, and I cannot pass over this question in silence. I read somewhere lately that it was 'a piece of pitiful sophistry unworthy of serious and honest thinkers' to argue that, while such stories are not historical they are 'true in some symbolic or metaphorical sense'.

For my own part I should want to distinguish. I do not think it has been reserved for our own generation to discover for the first time all the realities of the world and human nature, and I still find in some of the untrue stories of the past what seems to me to be truth about the world and Man. Thus the Creation story in Genesis—the later one that stands first in our Bible—is no doubt wrong in many of its details; but it makes creation a shaping process and recognizes stages and insists that the whole is good; and again, it depicts Man as the last of the stages—all else as it were as preparatory and subordinate to the production of that which most closely represents and embodies the creative principle that has been at work, One in whom its image and likeness is expressed. There is a great deal there of truth about the world and Man and Man's task in the world as modern Science conceives it. And if you admit Origen's gloss on the Hebrew, namely, that Man is made in the image of GOD to attain to His likeness, you have a complete religious estimate of the meaning and purpose of life.

Or again to take a story where the facts at their face value are more fundamentally wrong—the story of the Garden of Eden and the Fall of Man. We know that the picture of primitive Man's condition which that story gives is false. There never was a state of harmony or a golden age from which he fell. His whole history has been one of moral conflict, his primary animal instincts always active within him. There can be no question of restoration of what has never been.

But the knowledge of the past we have today justifies us in believing that the process of the world is somehow directed to the attainment of higher quality of being and existence than has yet been realized.

No doubt the story originated in Man's dissatisfaction with himself and his environment, his sense of his own capacity and incapacity; and it is thoroughly pessimistic. The flaming sword which turned every way keeps the way of the tree of life.

Yet, though it offers no hope of attainment, the story does tell what the way is. There may be things good for food and pleasant to the eye and to be desired to make one wise, on the one side, and on the other the consciousness that they are things forbidden. This consciousness is already there in the story. It is not really primitive Man with which it deals, but Man at a stage at which his higher and his lower instincts are already drawing him different ways and he is able to choose; and he chooses the way of satisfaction of the desire which he feels at the moment.

I do not think it is 'a piece of pitiful sophistry' to say that the story is true in a symbolic sense, that it has the truth of a parable.

The truth, I have no doubt—like all the approximations to truth which we are able to make—was an induction from a good deal of experience of human nature and life in the world. The inventor of the story knew what the moral conflict is for Man. And it 'happens' that the gist of his story is in harmony with the evolutionary view of Man's history which sees it as trending to the production of higher quality of life, and also with the sanest ethical teaching of today. For that teaching does not regard static ignorance or innocence as goodness, but finds morality to consist in the ever-active direction of all the instincts to the higher ends and interests of the individual and the race.

Of course we should prefer not to have to represent the command as coming from outside, but to treat the urge to higher life as the bidding of Man's own nature. From the beginning there is that within him which points him to a good in the future for the sake of which he must forgo the satisfaction of the moment.

But we are still far from dispensing with the idea of commands and laws imposed on us; and if we believe that the order of the world is moral as well as rational, we affirm that there are sanctions of a kind that it is imperative upon the individual to observe, if he is to keep his proper place in the whole to which by his very constitution he belongs. Certainly on the evolutionist conception there is a bidding of Nature to every constituent of the whole to be its best and to become better than it is.

I have taken examples of very old folk-tales. The pity is that, just because they were incorporated in our sacred Scriptures, they came to be regarded as intended to give authoritative information about questions which we call 'scientific', instead of being taken as religious valuations of the world and Man's place in it. I have no doubt that the spirit which was at work in making them—the spirit at work in almost all religious legend and literature—was at work also behind, if not actually in, the composition of our own specially Christian Scriptures. I have no doubt that some of the stories of our Gospels have their origin in the attempt to explain human experiences of an impressive and elusive kind by reference to powers and activities of a higher order than the known and natural. There was an established fashion in these matters, which still survives among those who have not become wholly habituated to the fashion of thought which has gradually spread since Copernicus and Newton and Darwin. And so the unknown quantity of which His contemporaries were aware in Jesus was accounted for by stories such as that of the Nativity; and some of His own experiences and their experiences in connexion with Him—the elusive quality of which ordinary measures could not cope with—experiences of which nowadays we should try to find a psychic account, were described in terms of events or occurrences of a wonderful character in the sphere of sense and sight and sound.

To dismiss these stories as worthless, when we are seeking a true valuation of Jesus Himself and the whole experience of which He was the centre, is to shut one's eyes to some of the bits of evidence we have about Him and the impression He produced. It is not the mark of a scientific enquirer to do so. It is not 'pitiful sophistry' to use these stories as evidence of the kind

I have indicated in making up our account of Jesus and the Gospel history. They come to us in the vesture of fairyland, or from the realm of poetry and picture; but experience of men and women like ourselves underlies them, and they help us to estimate the character and quality of that experience.

But, on the other hand, we are not entitled to allow them to control our conception of the relation of GOD to the universe, of the course of Nature, or of the methods in which He is actually manifested in the cosmic process and human history. We are not entitled to use them to buttress old ideas of breaks and intrusions and interpositions from outside. They are not 'symbolic' of 'truth' in this respect—no more so than the old idea of creation of species after species out of nothing is symbolic of the theory of natural selection.

Common human experience seems, indeed, to give a large measure of support to a theology of catastrophe and crisis. Breaks in our lives, sudden 'intrusions' of various kinds, do often happen. They are the obvious facts that anyone can see. A theology of the kind with which we are familiar corresponds to them. Any true *rationale* of life must include them in its survey. But whereas no student of the Natural Sciences is hindered on his way to knowledge of his subject by Ptolemaeus or any other scientific 'authority' of the past—Newton yields to Einstein, Darwinism in some respects to the suggestions of later biological research—Christians today are hindered on their way to a true valuation of the world and human life by the fact that their chief leaders and theologians of the past fitted their religious experience into the framework of the ideas that were current before the modern era of Science began.

Dr Inge has said that 'miracles must...be relegated to the sphere of pious opinion'. I am wholly with him in what I understand he meant, but I cannot think that the word 'pious' can be applied properly to the opinion that the physical portents which are recorded in connexion with the origins of the Christian Religion really took place as recorded. I know that when Athanasius wrote his *Life of Anthony*, he included stories of miracles which he regarded as well attested, and others that were less well attested; and of the latter he said that it was 'more pious' to believe them. And this religious temper and disposition, this line of belief, has been continuous among Christians from the angels of the Nativity story to the angels of the story of Mons. But I must affirm my conviction that it can never be a mark of piety to believe in any particular miracle recorded, in the past or in the present, when explanations of the origin of the belief are forthcoming that do not involve ideas about the universe and Man's life-history in it and GOD's ways of working out His purposes, that our general knowledge today does not confirm.

It is not religious to ignore the revelation in all these respects that has come to our generation through the patient and exacting work of seekers after truth in many directions. There is more of religion in the wisdom of Rabbi Ben Ezra—

> Here, work enough to watch
> The Master work and catch
> Hints of the proper craft, tricks of the tool's true play.

It was no doubt 'Victorian' to say—

> There lives more faith in honest doubt,
> Believe me, than in half the creeds.

But today it may be the part of the highest faith to repudiate and disown all those religious pictures of the past which pourtray ideas about GOD and the world and Man that nothing that we really know justifies us in harbouring.

We are as much responsible for what we believe as for what we do not believe, and the pictures of the past to which I have referred are in conflict alike with ethical and with theological truth as they present themselves to us today.

But let us turn from such constituents of so-called Christian Theology as those for which Evolution has no room and dwell on the construction of the world it gives us.

I have not propounded any exact definition of the term. I do not suppose it is necessary here to say that I am not using it in its literal sense, as it was used by Leibniz, to mean an unfolding from within, so that nothing could be evolved which was not first involved, but in the sense in which it is used in all scientific thought today—a sense quite different. The science of biology offers us the best illustrations of the process. The old idea was that the perfect organism was already existent in the germ or the embryo, preformed in all its parts, compressed as it were together and gradually unrolled and expanded. Everything was there to begin with. It is against this idea that most modern objections to the theory of Evolution are still directed. But no one works with this conception now.

'The parts of an organism are not thought of...as present in any sense in the embryo, but as gradually organized one after another in due order, so that a product results which was *not* preformed in the germ.'[1] There is, indeed, in every 'thing' the capacity for becoming what it does become, but only by combination with a multitude of other 'things', each of which has the capacity of contributing what is needed for the product that ensues. Each such formation is genuinely new. It is reached by a synthesis of existing constituents, and such synthesis is creative.

More exact descriptions of what is meant are given by the terms 'epigenesis' and 'creative synthesis'.

But Science suffers the same fate as Theology—we can exchange condolences. As knowledge advances it has to stretch out its old terms and fill them with new meaning. And, as a description of all the facts of the world and life revealed by recent investigation in all the spheres of the Natural Sciences—especially biology and anthropology which touch us all most closely, the term 'Evolution' stands for the view that the process by which things have come to be what they are, and are always becoming what they are going to be, is one of continuous organization, so that 'at every stage "objects of a higher order" are attained, and these in turn serve as the constituents of a further synthesis'.

Descriptions of the facts in physico-chemical or mechanistic terms, which were regarded as sufficient

[1] G. Dawes Hicks art. 'James Ward and his philosophical approach to Theism' *Hibbert Journal* Oct. 1925 (vol. xxiv p. 58) from which I have drawn phrases and some sentences.

till recently, are now less in favour. A new biological orthodoxy is forming, which holds that the facts that can be observed indicate at lower stages something like what we know as intention and purpose, a kind of dim sense of something desirable to be achieved, a trend towards a goal, a making for a higher organism in response to some inherent urge.

Of course the 'argument from design' which figured largely in proofs of the Being of GOD is discredited, in the sense of the old believer who found proof of the providence of GOD in the fact that He had made great rivers to flow through cities. But if we cannot believe in any such neat pattern of everything that was to be, preformed and pre-existing in the mind of a great Designer and Artificer, All-wise and All-good; if we are compelled to admit that much of what we can see looks more like reckless experiment of One who does not know what He really wants or lacks the means to achieve it; yet the evidence now available points clearly to a continuous process of creative synthesis productive of higher orders of being from the amoeba to Man. All the different species of other animals known to us appear as highly specialized forms as it were of some particular ingredient needed at some stage or other for the making of Man. That is to say, they seem to be in origin by-products of one continuous process. Whatever in them was wanted for the making of Man was absorbed into the main stock of which Man was the outcome. And then ensued, for better or for worse, the specializations that we know, some of which, being overspecialized and unable to cope with new conditions, became extinct, while others

71

degenerated to still lower forms, and yet others continued to minister, from outside, to the maintenance and further developement of the main stock. So that Man still possesses some of the characteristics of all other animals, while he is the least specialized of all of them and still capable of developements from which they are precluded.

That, as I read it, is the picture Evolution sets before us. And when the process is seen on this large scale, and when we bring to account the finding of our modern biologists, it does at least suggest to us Design.

If design there be, it must be exhibited most fully in Man, and the true intention of the process must be seen in the specifically human world, to the production of which all the earlier stages made their appropriate contribution.

When we survey the history of Man, we find that what the creative synthesis produces is not so much new entities as new values.[1] And the values produced in turn tend not only to be conserved but to lead to higher values—intellectual, aesthetic, moral—worthier forms and loftier ideals. It is a fact that there have emerged in the course of the process higher forms of Reason, Beauty, Goodness. And a process of which these are the outcome is a spiritual process.

'Science' deals only with what has been and what is. It does not prophesy. But from the evidence of the past it is a reasonable inference that these spiritual values, or whatever it is of which they are the expression, will become the dominant factors, and are in their highest forms the ultimate goal, of the process.

[1] G. Dawes Hicks *loc. cit.*

72

Science describes. It does not interpret. It makes no use of the hypothesis of GOD. But when we seek an interpretation, that hypothesis and the Johannine doctrine of Incarnation seem to account for the facts as Science describes them.

The standard of measure is not quantity but quality. Quality is always more elusive, less easy to measure, than quantity. But as it seems more fugitive, so it is also more diffusive. The sensitive catch it and spread it in turn. It was the new quality of the thought and character and life of Jesus that impressed itself on those who knew and heard of Him. They caught it from Him, because they were so constituted that they could. They had in their own being, waiting to be aroused, the factors which were dominant in His. It came as a new experience to them, giving them new conceptions of GOD and of themselves. It was a revelation of GOD and of Man, made in the drama of human life, with Jesus as chief *persona dramatis*, but only chief among many.

All theologies are Man's own rationalizations of the experience of Man. We have had many such rationalizations of what is called Christian experience. I wish that in this long lecture I could have better prepared the way for the suggestion with which I must now conclude. It is that, while the evolutionist revelation of our own times puts out of court much that has passed as Christian theology, it supports the Johannine rationalization summed up in the words 'Logos' and 'Incarnation'. It supports the idea that the whole process is one in which spirit is ordering and organizing towards the production of higher orders of being, higher qualities of life. And as long as the quality of life exhibited in Jesus is the highest we know, it is truth for us to regard Him as representing the highest factor of the whole scheme become dominant. With our belief that that highest factor is GOD, we see Him as GOD manifest under the conditions of human life. He shews the Divine purpose and plan, and it is only in so far as His attitude to life, His estimate of values, His temper, become dominant among men that the kingdom of heaven can be established in us and so in the world. And the kingdom of heaven in the world is the best ordering of human society that is attainable at the moment with a view to the perfect order that is to be—the society of perfected human personality in being.

V

EVOLUTION AND INCARNATION[1]

We put these two familiar words side by side, and as we look at them together we are reminded at once that one of Man's great characteristics is his capacity for artistry, his power of making pictures. Carlyle defined man as a tool-using animal, but that is a characteristic we share with some of our distant cousins among the apes. Man alone, so far as we know, draws pictures of the things he sees and can keep them by him to remind him of them. So writing began and all that the power of writing carries in its train. We picture our experience, we think in pictures, and it is only by pictures that we can express ourselves.

The Egyptian hieroglyphics are at the beginning of what we know as human civilization, and after six thousand years of its wonderful achievements it is still only pictures we can get.

Evolution is the hieroglyphic of Natural Science, and Incarnation the hieroglyphic of Christian Theology. Conceivably we might have better symbols of all the facts and processes of which either term is our description. But that thought suggests another which we need to have with us as a constant reminder. It is not our way to be always inventing new terms. When we have once devised our hieroglyphic, we keep it if we possibly can. We stretch it out to include the new ideas or the new knowledge that longer or wider

[1] A paper read to a Clerical Society in Birmingham in 1925.

experience brings. We infuse, as it were, fresh content and meaning into the older term. It is a very convenient way of maintaining continuity—in fact it is the way of life, we can hardly help ourselves: and it disguises from us the extent to which our environment has changed. We keep the old term. It comes to be generally received and used in a new sense, and it is only the student of the history of words and ideas and culture in general who is conscious of the difference.

No student or exponent of either the Christian Religion or Christian Theology can be at ease unless he realizes how largely he is dealing with pictures. Most of them are very old, some of them belonging to the earliest culture of Egypt or Babylonia, only a little bit retouched (or moralized if you will) in our Christian Tradition—such pictures as those of the Creation and the Fall of Man in Genesis. And others, such as we have in our Gospels, though they are less old, are yet quite as remote as the older ones from everything that makes up the cultural environment of our own times, all of them reflecting just the same stage or level of popular science. In this respect— I mean in the way of picturing experience—there is no dividing line between the Old and the New Testaments, and a Church which includes both in its canon of truth, and binds Genesis and Daniel and Jonah and Acts and John in a single volume, cannot for ever maintain different methods of interpretation in its different parts. The problem how to teach the Bible today to people, young or old, who accept as a matter of course our modern knowledge of the universe and

Man's history in it, can only be met, I believe, from the point of view which sees the Bible as a great picture-book of Man's religious experience and seeks through the medium of the pictures to arouse or quicken or confirm the capacity in us all for entering into the same experience and relating it to our own personalities and lives. Pictures of something real. I might say 'fairy-tales,' except that the fairy-tale is not usually of anything actually experienced or conceived as even possibly happening, whereas the picture is an attempt to pourtray on canvas or in word an idea of something which has formed part of the man's experience, which he wishes to describe to himself and tell to others.

Some of our greatest theologians from the beginning have used what at their face value are narratives of fact—incident and happening—in this way as pictures.

See, for example, how St John quietly brushes away as it were the pictures of the way in which Jesus came down from heaven into the world and the way in which He is to come again in the future on the clouds of heaven, replacing the one by his doctrine of the Logos and the other by his doctrine of the Spirit, of the judgement that is instant and immediate, and the eternal life that is a way of living now. Or see again how he strengthens the lines and intensifies the colour of all the narratives of miracles that he records, so as to make them more vivid pictures of the actual inward experience of light and life and truth which he found in the conviction that Jesus was the Christ, the Son of God, the very Logos incarnate, the manifestation of the Divine activity which always was and is and will be.

Other theologians after him may be found who treated the religious truth, the reality, described as something other than the plain implications of the story. The allegorical method of interpretation, no doubt, has often run wild. No doubt, it was a gain to call men back from it to the plain and historical meaning of the text. And yet it may come to be seen, more widely than it is at present, that the real history to be recovered from many of our narratives, the truth underlying many of our doctrines, is not what they seem to affirm in their graphic description and their terse and balanced definitions, but something deeper of which they are only a kind of hieroglyphic.

Christians are pledged, irrevocably as it seems to me, to the position that it is in human history that they are to see the clearest manifestation of GOD— human history in its comprehensive range from the beginning to the end. They are pledged to the interpretation of all that history as leading up to an end the character of which is indicated by the distinction that Man, in the course of his experience, has learnt to draw between his own different needs and wants and desires and aims. The fact that he can make the valuation 'good', and subordinate an obvious good of the moment to a more permanent or ultimate good, and that he can even renounce altogether the momentary good and choose instead of it a course involving hardship and effort and pain—this is itself an indication, both for individuals and for groups, of a teleology of human nature, of which Man is in some measure conscious. And at least the quality of the end that is to be is shewn by the emergence out of the actual conditions of Man's life of these moral and spiritual values. They are not imposed from without, but they arise from within his own nature and are the output of himself: they are his own estimates of the really good, and in the course of his history these estimates remove him farther and farther from his early ancestry in a steady moral and spiritual ascent. It is just in this history of Man's progress that we find GOD manifested, and using personal terms as we must, a plan or purpose being worked out—a scheme of things through all the ages that have been and are to be, through different races and individuals in them at different times, and of course at present especially through the Nordic race.

And we are pledged to the position that the fullest manifestation of GOD and this purpose of His—the real meaning of human life and the truth of things so far as Man is concerned—was made in the experience of Jesus and the men and women most closely associated with Him in His life.

I have said deliberately the experience of Jesus, 'the man Jesus'. It is on this that we depend, the experience of which Jesus Himself was the subject, as one 'born of a woman' at a particular moment in the whole historic process, in whose experience we see nothing pathological, but the outcome of the whole process in which we recognize the Divine purpose to produce the perfect man—the ἄνθρωπος τέλειος, *Homo perfectus* of our definitions—the man complete in all his parts, whole and healthy. I suppose there is no

79

fact in the history of Man more certain than the emergence of Jesus and the experience of which He was subject and centre; nor is anything more natural than that the narratives of that experience should have assumed the form we know. Our Gospels come to us from a Church already in existence; stories of the kind they contain were probably told from the beginning and believed, and no doubt down almost to our own times the Christian Faith for the mass of its adherents has rested on the evidence of direct supernatural intervention to which these stories literally understood bear witness. Our whole theological system is based on the supposition of a gulf between the natural and the supernatural, the human and the divine, which can only be bridged by a series of new creative acts of GOD. Our formal doctrine of the Person of Christ proclaims the permanent distinction of the Two Natures even when combined in Him. It is a story of discontinuities and gaps in the universe itself and in all human experience. And yet the experience of Jesus Himself which the synoptic Gospels set before us is a unity. It is our theologians who have split it up into parts that are labelled respectively human and divine. It is to this unity that we have to return if we are to come to terms in our Theology with all the findings of modern Science of which the term Evolution is the label.

I had chosen the subject 'Evolution and Incarnation' earlier in the year because it has long been my conviction that our Theology as a whole must be brought into line with the facts about the universe and Man's place and history in it that are common knowledge today, just as our Theology when it was formed was in line with what was common knowledge then. A month or two later I received from Dr J. M. Wilson, Canon of Worcester, an offprint of a chapter he was contributing to a collective work by experts in the various branches of the Natural Sciences designed to shew the present state of knowledge, the overwhelming consensus as to the main facts and the still remaining uncertainties as to some of the factors of the process. Dr Wilson's chapter is entitled 'The religious effect of the idea of Evolution'. It is a persuasive plea for full recognition of the new knowledge as being for our times no less than a new revelation of the truth, that gives us an evangel able to grip, coming in some real sense as 'news'—such as one of the Archbishops' Committees said was wanted if the Church was to obtain a hearing from educated people today. Dr Wilson wrote his chapter without seeing the rest of the book, but he has kept himself through a long life well informed about the developements of the Sciences since the days when he was Senior Wrangler and Science Master at Rugby. Having read what the specialists have to say, I think that Dr Wilson's conclusions are justified and that, when we abandon the dualism that pervades our Theology and recognize the unity and continuity that Science proclaims, we can have a doctrine of the significance of Jesus which the evolutionist would not quarrel with, the theologian could still describe as a doctrine of Incarnation, and Religion would find adequate to its deepest and purest demands.

It would, of course, take far too long to describe in detail the characteristics of such a new theology. I must keep as closely as possible to my title Evolution and

Incarnation, or the effect of the idea of Evolution on our doctrine of the Incarnation, and that doctrine especially as regards the relation between Man and GOD. And it is of course the new Science of which we have to take account, the Science of today rather than of forty years ago, and particularly the modern Biology. For, as we all know, there has been a marked change of attitude.

Like the famous French astronomer, the Science of today makes no use of the hypothesis of GOD—no more than did the Science of Huxley's day. But whereas it used to be thought that a complete description—or, when the word was used loosely, as it generally was, an 'explanation'—of the phenomena known to biologists could be given in mechanistic terms, some leading biologists today no longer share that opinion. They think, on the contrary, that the facts they observe indicate something more, something like a kind of incipient consciousness and purpose, and that the mere description is not complete unless it includes this kind of 'x' or unknown factor. This new view has not yet established itself as orthodox in Science, though it is the view of the writers on the subject in the new volume *Evolution*. But scientific orthodoxy now, in contrast with its earlier position, while still insisting on its *description* of processes as mechanical, definitely disclaims the idea that it is concerned with the task of explanation. And so it leaves the way open to the philosopher or theologian. Theirs is the business of explanation, of exploring the realm of meaning, of giving, if they can, some comprehensive interpretation of the facts. Only, as I understand, Science would insist that the philosophy or the theology should be consistent with its own findings. And that I think we must concede.

What it finds is a world that has been as it were by some kind of innate capacity making itself for millions of years from an unorganized multitude of atoms into the cosmos we know, by processes that have been continuous even if, after so great a lapse of time, the stages cannot always be traced. There is still a gap between what we have been accustomed to call 'animate' and 'inanimate' Nature, but the evidence that has been collected on either side of the gap seems to warrant the view that the *onus probandi* now lies on those who assert discontinuity between the atom and the living thing. At all events from the amoeba to Man there has been a continuous ascent in the scale of life. It is not denied that in the process what is genuinely new comes to be. The word Evolution in the hands of its scientific exponents today has lost its literal meaning and is used like 'epigenesis' or 'creative synthesis'. But the emergence of the new would be accounted for by the latent capacity in the organism and its environment, no intrusion from without the universe being required for the production of the newness. The creative capacity is within the universe and its factors, and the newness is produced by new combinations or arrangements of them by which higher orders are effected and these in turn lead on to others.

This is perhaps a sufficient survey of the findings of Science for our purpose today. At least it states the two main conclusions: (1) the unity and continuity of the whole process of which Man is the highest product we know, and (2) that the process is one from lower to higher orders of being, that there is a manifest urge or trend or tendency within the process towards something not yet attained.

Some biologists are so anxious to keep their Science free from any terms implying judgements of value that they would not admit the word 'higher' which I have just used. They would only say 'more complex' or 'more fitted to its environment'. And because 'progress' usually has some moral connotation, they would not describe the course of Evolution as one of progress. But as it is the world in relation to ourselves that we are concerned with, and especially the human part of it, I think we are justified in taking the findings of Science to mean that there is an inherent trend in the universe not only to the conservation of what already is (self-preservation) but also to the attainment of what is better than has yet been. We must consider Man the highest that has yet been attained, and as his progress has been marked peculiarly by the greater developement of his spiritual rather than his physical capacities, we are justified in regarding those character-istics of Man—the things of the mind or the spirit—as the highest values that the process has produced.

A biologist who lets himself stray beyond his own scientific domain has not restrained himself from speaking of 'Love' as the goal of Evolution. And a philosopher of the most evolutionist type has argued at length his interpretation of the whole universe as tending to the production of higher and higher qualities, using the term 'Deity' to describe the higher quality ahead that is always to be achieved.

How then does our Christian Theology stand in relation to such Science as this? One *caveat* before we answer. We are not entitled to pick and choose among the conclusions presented to us in the closely coherent scheme of Evolution. We may not accept what favours our traditional ideas and reject or ignore what tells against them. We may not claim Science on our side where it leaves us an open field and at the same time occupy ground it has closely barred against us.

We bring to bear at once, of course, our concept of GOD as ground of all being and we see the whole process as the gradual and progressive realization of a Divine purpose and end. Philosophy forbids us to say that intrusions from without our world cannot happen, but Evolution claims to have discovered an orderly and continuous process at work within it. The familiar antithesis natural and supernatural disappears—the 'natural' is the way in which the Divine purpose is being realized. If we picture some aspects of our experience as natural and some as supernatural, it is only a logical distinction of our own making. There is no dualism. GOD is in the process, indwelling. The whole universe is not merely the scene of His operations but a manifestation of Him, in all the stages of its evolution. The whole is Incarnation.

At this point I may be allowed to read to you a short summary of the main points in Dr Wilson's paper, partly because I wish to introduce it to those who have not read it and to say that they will find in it a simplicity and a religious fervour which will I am sure make it attractive. It is only a suggestion of Dr Wilson's chief points that can be offered here.

THE WAY OF MODERNISM

The starting point in the conception of GOD must be the human spirit. We must seek GOD within. As far as this globe is concerned, we men are the latest and highest result of the vast evolutionary process, and it is thus to the nature of man that we must look for the plainest indications of its purpose and meaning. Man must be the incipient vehicle of self-expression, the incarnation in some degree of the 'Unseen Creator Spirit Himself'. So the basis for Theology must be the study of GOD as Indwelling. 'GOD is not to be found by us in nature apart from man, but only as the Spirit dwelling in us'. The world of matter and life and spirit is one scene of orderly and continuous developement. There is no place in it for the old antinomies of a natural sphere and a supernatural sphere, or for the idea of an irruption of one sphere into the other. The whole process is Divine and we are led by a continuous chain from the lower to the higher in the evolution of human personality, till we come to the One Manifestation in which men have most fully found and seen and known GOD.

The traditional doctrines of Man and Sin and Atonement have been largely inherited from a primitive past, and have not yet been Christianized.

The great fact that stands out is that in the evolutionary process the emergence of good has taken place.

When, then, we consider our own specific doctrine of '*the* Incarnation', what has for a long time been in my own thought is that we might long ago have learnt from it just what Evolution has taught us. If we can get away for a moment from our Christological definitions, our dominant conviction is that Jesus is

86

at once a revelation to us of Man and of GOD. He shews us what Man is and what GOD is. I suppose in our sermons we tend to say rather what Man may be. But it is the whole person and life and experience of Jesus that constitutes the Revelation.

If you want to know the truth about GOD and the truth about Man and the real meaning of human life, its real values, *there* you have them—that has been the fundamental Christian claim and conviction. It is because of this that you must 'come to' Jesus, 'follow' Him, be 'conformed' to Him, so that you yourself may realize in the fellowship of life the truth about yourself. Whether you do this or not, it is the truth about yourself, and if you refuse it you are refusing the way of life.

There is a good deal in our New Testament, at all events in St Paul and St John, that suggests that they regarded the manifestation of Jesus as a manifestation of what had always been true about GOD and Man and their relations. The newness was the open realization. The prologue to the Fourth Gospel is perhaps the clearest expression of this thought, but the Epistles to the Romans and the Ephesians have phrases which are similar in meaning, and the Johannine Epistles and the Epistle to the Hebrews. If it is a plan or purpose which was to be achieved, yet all that had gone before was conceived as leading up to it and preparing the way. The eternal purpose was working all through the ages to the fullness of the times. Man was from the beginning destined for great things and high place, and the coming of Jesus was conceived from this point of view not as a sudden restoration of a state that once had been, and had been forfeited or lost, but as the realization in due order of a scheme of developement.

The early myth of the Fall of Man, like the Greek myth of the golden age, designed as an explanation of the discord in Man's experience, came in on the side of the scheme of Salvation to disarrange the implications of the wider doctrine, though there is a long line of theologians who held that all that was needed was accomplished by the Incarnation itself.

Today we know that there was no such golden age and no such Fall from a state of original righteousness, no pre-established harmony which the fault of Man destroyed, no loss of an original good. We know, on the contrary, that there has been a slow approximation to harmony, a gradual attainment bit by bit, with painful effort and many a relapse, a constant striving after a good, the character of which is only dimly understood after much experimentation and wandering down blind alleys. And so we are in a position in which we ought to slough most of the ideas which have given us doctrines of Atonement and conceptions of the nature of Salvation, of Sin and Heaven and Hell, which are as a matter of fact repellent to the moral sense of men today; and we ought to work out instead this doctrine of the *Christus consummator*—this rich vein in our original mine of doctrine which has been largely ignored in the past. If we do this, we shall have to lay more stress than has been usual on the experience of Jesus as the revelation of the truth about Man.

The *Ecce homo* factor of our doctrine will have to be much more pronounced; and, instead of all the old attempts to shew why it was that GOD became Man, why the need of Incarnation, why institutions and sacraments and all the rest, we shall take our idea of Incarnation back to the very beginning and trace the whole history of the world in the light of the end to be achieved.

So we interpret all the facts that the term Evolution stands for, through all the millions of years that they cover, as designed to lead up to the output of personal values. By GOD we mean the centre and source of the highest values, the constant activity of them all: and to ask if Jesus is GOD is to ask if He represents those highest values in human life.

From the evolutionary point of view He was the product of the past—He was on the highway of Man's history. But He was also new, an emergence of a new consciousness and new quality—a new type as it were of manhood, a new specialization. He is a new fact in life, and the realization of a potentiality is a definite achievement. We can say as confidently as on any theory of the Atonement that what He did, the things which He experienced, as well as what He was, won for mankind the possibility of that conscious communion and harmony with the Divine which constitutes their well-being or 'salvation' ($\sigma\omega\tau\eta\rho\iota\alpha$).

In all these connexions it is a comfort to know that any denial that Jesus was completely human is formal heresy, and that the doctrine of the Incarnation pledges those who hold it to the belief that human history and human life are to us at least the chief means of the manifestation of GOD. If we really could know all about Jesus, we should know all there is to

89

know of GOD and Man. Religion, as Religion, has no interest in GOD apart from Man. Its chief concern is with the GOD within Man.

The transactional elements in our doctrines are obviously imagery derived from common experience of life in the world: they are like our metaphors from space and time—Covenants and Commands, and all the rest of them; and they have their use in the world as it is and its historic—that is to say transactional—process, whether or no it be the case that space and time as much as deity belong to the stuff of reality, as our latest thorough-going evolutionary philosopher would have us believe.

It is human experience that concerns us chiefly, and when we regard it as the highest outcome yet achieved of the whole cosmic process, and that process itself as having Deity as its inherent urge and the emergence of Deity in its fullness as its goal, we know that everything that tends to the highest qualities of which we have experience, in human beings and human society, is an indication of what is ultimate and real. At all events in the present stage of the process it is in us and through us that the next stage must be reached. As far as we can see, it is to be by the prevalence of the type of manhood, character, personality, of which Jesus is the supreme representative for us. And we have as evangelical a task for ourselves and as evangelical a message for others, in the light of the new revelation which Evolution brings us, as our forefathers had with the knowledge of their days. I share Dr Wilson's opinion that we have in our hands what may prove to be a real evangel for the new age and may lead to a marked advance in the evolution of Man in his course from the animal to GOD.

We may still have our old pictures wherever they do not suggest ideas that are not true. But our doctrine of Man must have what we believe about Jesus as Man as its basis; Man is an incarnation of GOD. And our doctrine of GOD, His character and will and purpose, must be framed in accordance with the actual facts about the process of Evolution which, on any theistic hypothesis of creation of any kind, are the expression of that character and will and purpose.

VI

JESUS AS HUMAN AND DIVINE[1]

Our subject this morning is Jesus as 'both human and divine', or, as I should prefer to put it, 'the GOD-Man'. We do not ask the old question, *Cur Deus homo?* nor even 'How *can* this be?' But, accepting the fact of the *Deus homo*, we only ask: 'How was it, how is it so?' What were the conditions of the synthesis? How is it related to the facts of our experience, and what does it mean to us? To clear the ground I would start with two or three premisses, and the first of them is that 'orthodoxy', in beginning with GOD, began at the wrong end.

The personality of Jesus is for religion, and for science properly so-called, a perennial problem. The Christian who consciously looks to Him as Redeemer and Lord and Judge can leave the problem alone or acquiesce in the general opinion of his Church, clear-cut in expression but very vague in sense.

All Christian doctrine grows out of the puzzlement felt by the first generation of Christians. They knew He was a man in outward appearance and life, but there was something more which baffled them, and the doctrine that He was GOD as well as Man was an early result of reflexion on the facts of their actual experience.

In a recent controversy across the water, one of the protagonists said that he recognized the fact that Jesus was Man as well as GOD, but it didn't interest him: all he cared to know was how He was more than Man.

[1] A paper read at the Conference of Modern Churchmen held at Girton College, August 1923.

That was indeed the question which preoccupied the early Church—to such a degree that the manhood more and more receded behind the Godhead. Christian thought tended to begin at the unknown end. It was a Divine Person who had come into the world. God had been born as Man, without ceasing to be what He was before. This point of view presents us with a hopeless tangle of problems. Today, when in every department of investigation we begin with the relatively known and reason from what we find there to the unknown, it is Jesus as Man in His life in the world that we want to take as our starting point once again —as at the outset He was. That is what gives our modern study of Gospels and Gospel history its interest and importance. We know He was human, we believe He was also divine. It is by finding out how He was Man—what He was in His place in the historic process —that we may come to understand in what sense He was and is also GOD.

Parenthetically I would say: We must absolutely jettison the traditional doctrine that His personality was not human, but divine. To our modern categories of thought such a statement is a denial of the doctrine of the Incarnation. There is for us no such thing as human nature apart from human personality: the distinction that He was Man but not 'a' man, while it has deep religious value,[1] has ceased to be tenable.

[1] What I have in mind as the religious value, the truth, of this old distinction is retained and even enhanced for 'modernists' in the modern emphasis on the fullness of our Lord's humanity. For what is meant is that Jesus does not stand alone as 'a' man might be thought to stand, isolated from his fellows. He is one of them among them. He is identified with the whole experience of the

The personality of Jesus is human—He is 'whole' man even for Chalcedon: it is also divine for Christian faith and consciousness in all ages.

The question is one, primarily, for historical investigation. In this historical investigation I can make no use of the traditional beliefs in either His miraculous birth or His personal pre-existence. Both beliefs, no doubt, are of high religious value which Christianity must conserve. The former, like all docetic theories, stands for the fact of something 'new' in human experience; but we know enough of the order of Nature now to discredit the ancient idea that the new can only come about by a break in the continuity of the order of Nature, and I can only regard this idea of miraculous birth as aetiological and honorific—in those days as natural and reasonable a way of accounting for a great personality and the experience of which Jesus was the cause and the centre, as it would be unnatural and irrational[1] today. The latter belief, which is itself an inference from belief in His Godhead,

race, within it, not outside it as an individual by himself. He is a member of the group, the family, of men, not separated and not separable from it. So like Adam He is representative—the one of the old, the other of the new, moral life of mankind. Without breach in continuity or solidarity a new character is given to the race, a new racial unity is established: a new type, to become endemic and spread its contagion through the whole race.

[1] The writer of this paper was asked what he meant in this connexion by 'irrational', and replied that he should call a belief 'irrational' in any age if it could not be related to the generally accepted *Welt-anschauung* of the period or the knowledge or best thought or theory with regard to the matter in question at the particular time. Such a belief might therefore be rational at one time and irrational at another, according to its cultural or scientific *milieu*.

suggests to us that what was made manifest in the personality and life of Jesus was a manifestation in space and time of a reality super-temporal, super-historic. I shall return to this point at the end of my paper.

We must first get our basis in the historical conditions of the manifestation itself, the conditions precedent and actual; and though I have little to add to what Mr Emmet said, I must say it in my own way.

The conditions precedent include the facts of the whole of the long life-history of Man, but more particularly the special cultural history of the race to which Jesus κατὰ σάρκα belonged—all his own inheritance of national religion and ideas of psalmists, prophets, and apocalyptists, which formed the *substratum* of His own personal conscious experience. I am quite willing to use the term 'subconsciousness' instead of *substratum* if it be understood that this subconsciousness is thoroughly natural and human. He came into the world with this inheritance, or at any rate it fashioned Him from the moment of His birth and provided the channels of His thought, even though He might cut some new ones or divert and give a new direction to the old.

If we give full weight to this cultural inheritance as it is known to us today, we find in Jesus a newness and originality of thought which is selective and evolutionary, shewing that He was on a higher plane and carrying us with Him, in the manner of the saying attributed to Him about the Law, 'I am not come to destroy, but to fulfil'. By His rejection of some old ideas and the emphasis of His selection, He becomes

95

the creator of something new in the history of religion: a new conception of GOD and of Man and of the relations existing ('potentially', perhaps, but that is to say for all religion *really* existing) between them, of the essential character of GOD and the meaning and purpose of human life.

He was conscious of this newness. He was the first man to know GOD as He really is. To others discoveries have come, conceived by them as revelations of reality or truth, granted, given: they have heard the authentic voice or seen things as they are. Often they are eager to tell the world, they must 'give' to others what has been 'given' to them: but the world is dull of hearing, and only a few will listen. Jesus does not stand alone in this respect: He casts a kind of halo on a great company before Him and after Him. In the history of human thought there are instances of men who have made discoveries that remain for ever associated with their names: through them 'truth', the reality of the things in question, was revealed to the world.

Jesus was also conscious of 'mission'. He had been chosen by GOD to be the first man to know Him and reveal Him to others, and manifest in His own person GOD's character and purpose by the tenour and purpose of His own life. His sense of mission grew through the course of His own experience more specialized. Nothing was to be allowed to interfere with His fulfilment of this mission. This is a high estimate of self—His significance and His life—in relation to GOD and to Man and the world. He has in His own esteem a unique part to play in the ever-moving Drama of the Ages and a central position in the mind and purpose of God.

Is this consciousness of self other than human? It is to the human environment, the relatively known, that we must look first. *Causae non sunt multiplicandae praeter necessitatem.* Is a really new factor necessary to produce and account for this kind of consciousness?

When Marcion's docetic view of the Redeemer was met by the objection that by those who saw Him He was regarded as a man, he is said to have replied, '*satis erat illi conscientia sua*' (Tert. *de carne*, 3)—'His own knowledge of Himself was enough for Him'. Marcion meant He knew He wasn't a man. But even when the docetic theory was excluded, the great exponents of doctrine, and Christians in general, have assumed that He was conscious of Himself as divine. He knew that He was God: and our ecclesiastical theory of the Incarnation and interpretation of the Gospels proceeds on this assumption. I do not think it is in any way *either* justified by the evidence *or* required by the logic of the doctrine. I do not for a moment suppose that Jesus ever thought of Himself as God. Nor do I think that even the Fourth Gospel so represents Him: else, to cite one passage only, it would hardly have admitted the message sent through Mary to His brethren, 'I ascend unto my Father and your Father, and my God and your God' (Jn. xx 17)

Consciousness of being God was not one of the conditions of the *Deus homo*. The whole content of His consciousness is rightly styled 'unique', but it is human. There is no saying or act certainly His, and I think none in the Synoptic Gospels (if we except the narratives of the Nature Miracles) that could not come from a man of His lineage and convictions—the convictions themselves being only 'unique' in degree.

I think this reading of the facts has won fairly wide recognition among students today, who are no longer hypnotized by orthodox presuppositions. If we are to work with the orthodox theory of the Incarnation, I am sure we can only do so by making use of the conception of *kenosis*[1] to the full extent: the pre-existent Person must have so limited not only His power, but also His consciousness, as to be able to pass through the normal process of human life. He must have put so complete a restraint on memory that it could only act subconsciously without His being aware of His own prehistoric existence and life.

In my own thought on the subject I have occupied this position and expressed it, for example, in the prelection which begins and in the sermon which ends my little book on *The Faith of the Apostles' Creed*. But it is undoubtedly exposed to many of the objections brought against all *kenotic* theories, such as are marshalled in massive array in A. B. Bruce's book *The Humiliation of Christ*. And though it represents the utmost concession that orthodoxy can make to modernist demands, or the nearest approximation that tradition strictly interpreted can reach in its always unwilling, but always inevitable, attempt to come to terms with the thought of successive ages, I do not think it can be a permanently satisfying solution of the problem. It can only be a bridge from the past to the present, and we ought perhaps to be content if

[1] 'Self-emptying'—see *The Epistle to the Philippians* ii 6 ff.

most of our friends get on to it and stay there safely, refusing to follow the more active among us who are exploring the country beyond: that country which seems to promise us a habitation more permanent and a climate in which we can breathe more freely and win our souls by a venture costly, perhaps, but not to be refused by us. We do not expect a land flowing with milk and honey, and the Jericho whose walls have already fallen is behind us, though some are trying to build them again.

It is not, I am sure, to any theory of depotentiation of GOD that we can look to give us the conditions under which we can explain Jesus as both human and divine —the fact of the *Deus homo*. Nor could we hope to justify the theory from the mere facts of His life in the world apart from the experience known to us as the Resurrection and all that followed it. But when we attempt to place Him in the light of all our knowledge of what had been before and what has been since, and see exhibited in Him the real relations between GOD and Man and the key to the riddle of reality—and this is what the philosophy of the Incarnation sees in Him —then we are able to say what His being both divine and human means.

The primary and fundamental condition is the fact that the being of GOD and the being of Man are indissolubly interrelated. We are familiar with the idea of the 'eternal' generation of the Son (ἀεὶ γεννᾷ τὸν υἱὸν ὁ πατήρ). We have to apply the same conception to what we call the created world of finite intelligences. The Creator is not separated from His creatures: they do not exist apart from Him. They

99   7-2

have their origin in the will and love of GOD: they are the counterparts of that will and love, as necessary to the existence of GOD as He is to theirs. Neither is complete without the other. Language almost fails us, but GOD is always being actualized, fulfilled, expressed in Man; and Man only comes to full consciousness—the fullness of his potentiality—in GOD. It is not only that 'in Him we live and move and have our being', but also, however much bigger His being may be, it is true that 'in us He lives and moves and has His being'.

Of course we cannot appeal to our Lord's own words for more than hints of such an idea. But assuredly also we cannot for any of the forms the orthodox doctrine of the Incarnation has assumed. What is much more to the point is that it is He and His life—His experience as man in the world, His consciousness of Himself so far as we can read it with the new consciousness in us which He created—that suggests it. And though we can quote none of the standard expressions of Catholic doctrine for it, there has been much Christian thought that tends to support the belief that the historic process of human experience—to use modern terms—is in some real sense GOD's own experience.[1] He is the subject of it as well as we. We do not, I say, get much help from our technical statements of doctrine. Our technical definitions are frankly dualistic. They treat GOD and Man as two distinct real existences ('sub-

[1] Cf. G. Galloway 'The problem of the personality of GOD' in *Journ. of Religion* i 3 p. 305 'this supreme revelation [in Christ] has its presupposition in that wider activity of GOD in virtue of which he sustains all souls and works in and through them'.

stances'), each with its own special characteristics, which are incapable of being blended or fused into one, though in Jesus Christ they are so brought together and intimately related to each other that a 'union' of both can be spoken of.

A form of sound words is obtained by placing the centre of union in His person conceived of as prehistoric and divine and possessing a miraculous unifying power of holding together two distinct and disparate realities and becoming the subject of two sets of experiences which yet remain, in themselves, incongruous even while concurrent. This is to say, it is not professed that the experiences themselves are unified. The subject is one, but two distinct spheres of consciousness remain. And the fact that the unity conceived is beyond words and reason is registered by the decision for two wills and the rejection of the idea of one divine-human activity (θεανδρικὴ ἐγέργεια), as conceived by Dionysius the Areopagite and the Severians of the sixth century.

Our popular theology is indeed here in better case, and in this fact lies our better hope for the future. When we put all our traditional documents into their place in the archives of our religion for the use of our students only, to shew them how things have come to be what they are, to help them to get historical perspective: and when we go out into the market-place and speak with the man in the street, we are much more likely to be able to come to terms with him than we are with orthodoxy. Of course he thinks that GOD and Man are distinct—very properly (the dualism of our definitions is practically sound: the trouble is that

THE WAY OF MODERNISM

they make this practical dualism theoretic): but the man in the street is familiar with the belief that somehow or other Jesus Christ was both GOD and man, and he knows that he himself has much in common with Jesus as depicted in His life in the world, and is ready to believe that the something in himself of which he is at least dimly conscious as a 'not himself'—which he discerns in Jesus raised, as it were, to its highest power—may be at once really himself and GOD. He is in a position by no means to bring Jesus down to his own level, but to understand that he really has kinship with Him even in that something in virtue of which Christians style Him 'Lord' and 'GOD'.

It has always been the life-blood of common Christian religion that union with GOD was possible for man in and through Jesus, whether thought has rested primarily on what He did for us, or rather on what He was and is; and side by side with the thought of Him as Redeemer has run that of Revealer and Consummator. And in spite of the dichotomies of technical theology, some of the great theologians themselves who gave their minds to the question: How could these things be? found the answer in the fact that GOD was not only the source, but the continuous potency of man's life and being—the ground of his natural life as well as of the new life made possible for him by the Incarnation. The conception remains vague and attention is concentrated on the far-reaching and revolutionary effects of the Incarnation in renewing Man and opening out to him the path to his true destiny from which he had strayed. But when we use modern language and conceive of GOD as at once immanent and transcendent, and of personality in each of us as conditioned by and a reflection of the reality which is GOD: when we find the root of our personality in GOD, the infinite reservoir of consciousness from which our own trickling streams are drawn and fed, reservoir of all that we know as true and beautiful and good in instinct and purpose and achievement: then we recognize kinship with Him, kinship of very life and being, whether by His own *fiat*, or the gift of His love, or the eternal necessity of His being. We may go on contrasting our nature and His, and using the distinction between the natural and the supernatural, but in us—in our persons—there is already the super-natural blended with the natural, there is the sugges-tion of an Incarnation.

Baron Friedrich von Hügel is thinking on these lines. In an address given to junior members of the University of Oxford last year and published in the *Constructive Quarterly*, December 1922, under the title, 'Christianity and the Supernatural', he was at pains to bring home to his readers belief in 'the natural-supernatural character of human experience as a whole', and (as I understand) to suggest that we have in Jesus, the Christ, 'the supreme concrete example' of such a natural-supernatural experience, so that apprehending, as we must, that 'the supernatural en-dowment is very unequal amongst men', we find that there exists in this 'one particular human mind and will' 'one supremely rich, uniquely intimate union with GOD'. 'In this genuinely human mind and will, the series of all possible supernatural experience by man...reaches its implied goal and centre'. And he writes of 'a reality distinct from the apprehender, and yet a reality sufficiently like the human spirit, when thus supernaturally sustained and sublimated, to be recognized by this human spirit...as its living source, support, and end'.

Or again, 'Jesus...is declared to hold in His human mind and will as much of GOD, of GOD pure, as human nature, at its best and when most completely super-naturalized, can be made by GOD to hold, whilst re-maining genuine human nature still. And yet this same Jesus (though in this supremely heightened sense the Christ) remains thus also truly Jesus—that is, a human mind and human will bound to a human body, to sense stimulation, to history and institutions, to succession, time and space. He can thus be our Master and our Model, our Refuge and our Rest'.

That is a statement of one of the finest and most Christian minds of today. I find the conception of the Incarnation expressed in it essentially in harmony with the line of thought I have been following in this paper, and have expressed in other words in my little book, *The Faith of the Apostles' Creed.*

It is, I think, only from the point of view of the natural and supernatural as already blended in the being and life of Man, that we can attach meaning to the idea and the fact of Jesus Christ as the incarnate Son of GOD, the supreme example of Man in conscious dependence on and union with the source and stay of his life, finding the fullness of his personal potentiali-ties—the realization of Himself—by losing Himself in GOD, by persistent identification of thought, feeling, purpose, activity, with the highest, most pure and beneficent that Man had conceived, and by that very process carrying the achievement of the race a stage farther on, and by His personal attainment creating in the long history of human experience a new type of human personality in which we discern, as we could not otherwise have known it, the fulfilment of a design which aims at not simply throwing up from time to time an individual like Him, but producing a world-wide society of human persons fashioned after that type.

Along these lines of thought we have the Catholic and common conviction that Jesus was 'perfect man', the actualized ideal of man, man at the end of his evolution, complete; not that the manhood has been deified, nor yet again dehumanized (thoughts so abhorrent to Nestorius), but in virtue of its constitution *capax Dei*. And again, we have the substance of the Pauline thought of the summing up of all things in Christ which the insight of Irenaeus seized on and emphasized before Christian piety had fully re-coiled from the plain facts of the Gospel history as to the 'limitations' of the manhood.

All these convictions, of course, work with the idea of life as rational, with a purpose in view, an end to be attained, which is pictured as the will of a supreme personal intelligence. They are positive convictions and a complete negation of Hardy's idea of an unconscious will of the universe blindly at work, struggling in the dark, with just a possibility of attaining consciousness of beneficent purpose and goal and means to the end. On the other hand, they do not exclude the idea of a GOD who, in willing the world and personal intelligences and wills that were to be

105

faint copies of His own, capable of conflicting with each other and with His, willed struggle for Himself and them. He 'created' difficulties for Himself and them.

The idea of a prime Mover Himself unmoved, or of a GOD within whose Being there is nothing analogous to the insurgencies of human affections and emotions, is not Christian, though many Christians have had it.

The one and the many of non-Christian philosophy from the beginning until now meet in the GOD-Man reality implied in the fact of the Incarnation and the doctrine of the Trinity. Personality is something not in essence singular, but plural. Reality is represented ultimately by the Pauline 'All in All' ($\pi\acute{a}\nu\tau a$ $\grave{\epsilon}\nu$ $\pi\hat{a}\sigma\iota\nu$) —a plural phrase.

I think I have said enough now for the purpose of discussion; but you will expect something more than I have said about the traditional doctrine of the 'personal pre-existence' of our Lord. For St Paul, who seems to have believed in an ideal man or Messiah, stored away in the heavens, to be manifested in due season on earth, the conception was a natural, almost unconscious, inference from his belief that Jesus was Messiah. Those categories have no obvious relevance to knowledge and thought today.

Again, to early Christian religiosity, with its background of angels and daemons, its world of physics in which there was nothing that could not happen because no one knew how [or why] anything happened, the idea of the pre-existence of Jesus was an almost inevitable inference from the belief in His Godhead— an inference from an inference. GOD had sent His Son into the world to save it, and the Son had come of His own free will. 'He loved me and gave Himself for me': that is the authentic note of Christian faith and experience. And nothing can ever more convincingly commend to us the concept of GOD as Love than this picture of Father and Son alike and together agreeing in the great redeeming purpose and action. Any doctrine that can claim to be Christian must safeguard the conviction that the activity of redeeming love—the action of sacrifice—is the very centre of reality.

It is difficult to translate this picture into scientific theology without becoming tritheistic. Recently Dr Tennant has trenchantly exposed this difficulty in two articles in the *Constructive Quarterly* (June and September 1920). His conception of personality (like Dr McTaggart's in his article in Hastings' *E.R.E.*) seems to me to be atomistic and to exclude almost everything that we commonly associate with the term and value in one another. But I agree with him that the popular conception of the Trinity is tritheistic, and that those of us who allow ourselves to talk of the Christian conception of GOD as 'social' rather than 'individual' are exposed to the charge of talking metaphysical nonsense. Perhaps the best that can be said for our scientific theology is, that it provides us with a formula that gives some kind of coherence to the various aspects of our actual religious experience.

We may drop the category of 'substance', under cover of which the old orthodoxy could speak of 'ways' or 'modes' of existence—one being described as Father, one as Son, and one as Holy Spirit—a 'substance'

which had these three 'personal' and characteristic
activities: but we may not as Christians conceive of
the personality of GOD as less capacious and rich in
its activities and relationships—less subject of manifold
experience of the most profound and intimate order—
than our Christian forefathers represented by the
philosophical terms and the human analogies in which
their convictions and reflection were expressed. It is,
however, significant that it is on ethical rather than
metaphysical grounds that the theory of 'personal
pre-existence' is defended today by its only considerable champions[1]—quite a modern line of defence that
is congruous with the increasingly ethical tone of
ontological speculation and the current philosophy of
values. It is argued that the great sacrifice which the
belief that GOD is Love implies, which is manifested in
the life of the Incarnate, must belong to the very Being
of GOD. It must be pretemporal, prehistoric. The Son
Himself is involved in it, must share in it *ab initio*, in
person, not only in idea. The relationship Father and
Son, as representing the actuality of love and its inherent activity of sacrifice, must be rooted in the Being
of GOD. So the Son must be as eternally existent as
the Father. The religious value of the idea is obvious.
I do not think we can escape the logic of the argument
or entrench ourselves behind the thought of an ideal
existence outside Time in contrast with a real one in
Time.

But it must be observed that for scientific theology
the pre-existence of the Son is not really 'personal'

[1] E.g. H. R. Mackintosh in *The Person of Christ* pp. 445 ff. (as
indeed by A. B. Bruce, in *The Humiliation of Christ*, before him).

in the sense in which popular religion understands the term. By faith in GOD today we mean the conviction that Power and Love and Purpose are the characteristics of ultimate reality. And the Pauline conception of pre-existence, to which I have referred, may be found to have its true religious and scientific value for us as the expression of the conviction that the personality and life of Jesus was the crowning manifestation of this divine power and love and purpose: that in Him regarded as Redeemer was revealed in the fullness of time and actualized—or we might say evolved as the natural resultant in due sequence of the whole course of human experience and history to that moment— the ideal which was in GOD's mind in the creation of man. Where it is the eternal and inherent creativeness of GOD that is in action, the highest manifestation of it in human experience and history 'always' 'was'.

Or I would put it in another way and say: For love to be there must be subject and object, but there need not be reciprocation. If reality is really GOD and Man: if a world of finite intelligences is co-eternal with GOD, whether the world we know or another or many others, and if it is the externalization of Himself as it has been conceived as being; then the doctrine of the Incarnation means that the expression of Himself (thus externally in time in the world and Man) reached its plenitude in the man Jesus. He is the perfect expression in time and space of the personality of GOD: no sudden intrusion on the historic process, but its perfect product, the scion of many forefathers to be the firstborn of many brethren.

So, if I may end this long paper with an attempt to say as simply as possible what, on this conception of the conditions of the Incarnation, the Incarnation means, and put it personally, I should say that what my faith in the Godhead of Jesus means to me is that I believe that, in getting to know Him, I get to know GOD: that what He does for me, the at-one-ment of which He makes me conscious, is a divine work. Never does He cease to be man for me: the whole appeal He makes to me is through that which I have in common with Him; only when I regard Him as Man can I learn anything from Him. Yet what I learn from Him is GOD as well as Man. He becomes for me merged, as it were, in GOD, or identical with GOD. It is not that love for Him 'leads me on' to love for the Father He loved, but that in loving Him I believe I love the Father. If I am on His side, I am on GOD's side. If I truly serve Him, I am serving GOD. I am constantly left to my own devices as to ways and means of living in the world as it is on the lines He manifested and reveals. But so far as I can make His ideals and His values of life my own, I am sure I am doing the will of GOD. GOD stands to me for the highest values in life, and because I believe those values were actualized in the person and life of Jesus, I must use the title 'GOD' of Him.

When I take St Thomas' words, penetrating and personal as they are, and declare Jesus 'my Lord and my GOD', I am conscious that my categories of thought are not the same as those of a Tertullian or the Fathers of Nicaea or of Chalcedon, or of any ecclesiastical definitions down to the present day. I do not know exactly how to describe the *differentia*. It is not quite satisfactory to say that those definitions are conceived on lines of thought that are 'physical' and 'onto-logical' when they deal with the relation between Jesus and GOD; for those were the terms in which they described ultimate reality, and when I call Jesus GOD I mean to express the same relation between Him and reality. I think I mean quite as much as the Fourth Evangelist meant when he created the St Thomas narrative to become the classic expression of faith in the incredible, *credo quia impossibile*, and as he meant by the words he assigns to Jesus Himself: 'He that hath seen me, hath seen the Father'.

When our conception of reality has become essentially ethical, spiritual, personal, then our faith, our religion, must be expressed in terms of our own relation as persons to it: and when I say that the man Jesus is 'GOD', I mean that He is for me the index of my con-ception of GOD. I say 'He', because I mean not only His teaching, His own ideas about GOD, but also His life, His personality as a whole, as I learn it, primarily from the impression He made, so far as it can be in-ferred from the Gospels and the early religious ex-perience of which He was the centre.

It is not from anything that I know beforehand about GOD that I infer that Jesus is GOD incarnate. I know almost nothing about GOD's character apart from Jesus. But I attribute to GOD the character of Jesus. I say my conception of GOD is formed by my con-ception of Jesus. The GOD I recognize is a supreme 'person' like Jesus in all that makes 'personality'. In thinking of GOD personally as Jesus did and as we do,

I believe that I am, at all events, thinking along the lines of truth, in the right direction. So Jesus is the creator of my GOD. The relations into which I can enter with Jesus are for me relations with GOD. I know, of course, that I may be the victim of illusion; it is my faith that, through this estimate of Him, of His significance, I am in touch with reality.

§ VII

WHY WE BELIEVE IN JESUS CHRIST[1]

Why do we believe in Jesus Christ?

I take it that this question, propounded at this Conference, has in view the great shifting of the grounds of belief among educated Christians of our own generation. We believe in Jesus Christ. We believe that our house is built on rock. But so much of our old building has decayed, there are so many wings of it that have crumbled away, and so many rooms in which we cannot live, that we feel we need to examine again the foundations of the central block, the rooms of which seem never to have been unduly crowded. Have our central convictions about Jesus Christ a solid foundation?

Of the many ways along which an answer to this question might be approached—and no one here will expect to do more than approach an answer—I invite you this morning to explore two only. Both of them are ways of actual human experience, the one the way of our knowledge of ourselves as we are, and the other the way of knowledge of the history of the world and Man in the past.

Memories of childhood, of our earliest prayers and hymns, would lead most of us to the one main reason for our belief in Jesus Christ—none the less a good reason for us because if we had been born of Moslem

[1] A paper read at the Conference of Modern Churchmen held at Oxford, August 1925.

parents we should have had a similar reason for belief in Mohammed. Jesus was established in the environment in which we first came to consciousness, in a position mysterious and appealing. From Him and in Him first we caught the idea of the sacred in its most human and romantic form. We came to associate with Him all that is high and inspiring. Truth, Beauty, Goodness met in Him. Each is adorable, and in the Person in whom they meet we were taught to see GOD as by a mirror, the visible of the invisible. He became the centre of our religious ideas and experience. We were engaged once for all in a personal relationship to Him—the historical person who lived in the world, was put to death in the flesh, but is still alive in the spirit, ever ready to help us in all things good. He was to be our example, and through Him the power to follow it would come. Our loyalty was pledged. We were enlisted to be Christ's faithful soldiers and servants to our life's end.

And though we found, unconsciously, before we knew the words, how many compromises were accepted, how far ideals were from being realized in the world which thus enthroned Him; yet we learnt how this faith in Jesus Christ had inspired and directed the lives of men and women to ends and achievements which were obviously high and noble, and given them the double courage both to endure and to dare. And we have all had, in some degree, similar experience of our own. Our sense of sin has at least one of its roots here, and the return to allegiance redeems.

I would not use this experience in any merely pragmatic way. I am not asking you to consider the heart's desire or human needs or hopes. I would accept whatever light may be thrown by new investigations and new hypotheses on the nature of Man's personality and the processes by which it is shaped, however they be labelled. I am in no way concerned to distinguish sharply the objective and the subjective, the divine and the human. It is human experience, human awareness, perception, apprehension with which we have to deal: subject and environment. I am only concerned to say that if in the special experience to which I am referring Jesus Christ stands for the spiritual values which His life represents—and His life is His own personal experience—then the fact that this experience has been ever since continuously and persistently renewed again and again is very strong evidence that the truth about the world and Man is to be found in this direction. Jesus does not stand as an isolated phenomenon in human life. Historically he was in line with Hebrew prophets and psalmists, and such men as could conceive of the world as coming into being by the action of the Spirit of God on already existing matter and, by successive stages, culminating in Man in the image of God after His likeness, from chaos to cosmos, from the green grass to Man; and yet further, from their standpoint of experience in a world which seemed to be all askew, could conceive of the coming of One who would put all right. And again historically there is an innumerable company of men and women who have been His spiritual kin, and in all varieties of conditions and in many different ways of life have convinced themselves that the real values, the inner or real meaning of life, the truth of

things, is to be found where He found it. That is the
way to win your soul.

My argument is that a massive array of human experience—the most real thing we know—supports the
reading of the meaning of the world which we infer
in its general character from what we know of the
thought and life of Jesus.

The question is whether Man's true constitution and
nature is really represented by Jesus, and the argument is that the wide response which this representation arouses is a good reason for believing it to be true.
The *testimonium animae naturaliter Christianae* has gained
in cogency since Tertullian's and Augustine's time if
it be taken in this sense. The experience of Jesus is on
the highroad of the true course of man's life: it is not
pathological.

Let us put this argument in another way. Let us
take a characteristic and certainly genuine saying of
Jesus: 'Whosoever would save his life shall lose it;
and whosoever shall lose his life for my sake shall save
[*or* find] it'. The core of the Christian gospel of life is
there. The religious experience of Jesus is summed up
in it. Yet I do not believe that it is true because Jesus
said it, or on any authority from without. But, rather,
because Jesus said it, I believe in Jesus. It is because
saying after saying of His, action after action, His
attitude to life and its experiences, joy and sorrow
and pain and death, 'finds' me, if I may use Coleridge's
word, that I believe that what he says is the truth of
my own nature. In this respect He is the true Humanist. And because in this way I believe that His insight
into the values of human life and the reality of things

was true, I can use of Him in the third person such affirmations as the author of the Fourth Gospel puts in His own mouth—by what I hold to be a literary device that is also true interpretation of His significance and place in human history. He is the Way, the Life, the Truth; the Light of the World; the 'Resurrection', in the sense that to know Him is to know both GOD and Man: to be in fellowship with Him, in such wise that we share His spirit and have our lives directed by it, is to be living the true, the eternal, life.

If others of His own or other races and other tongues, before Him or independently of Him, discerned much of what we associate peculiarly with Him, that was no stumbling-block to early Christian apologists. The prologue to the Fourth Gospel, the Gospel of the Spirit, St Paul in a measure, Justin at his best, and Clement of Alexandria—to name but a few—recognized the Divine guiding of the human race as a whole and manifestations of it in individuals. And it is surely no stumbling-block to us to whom the appearance of discontinuity argues simply gaps in our knowledge or defects of observation. The originality, the newness, we find in Jesus is that of one to whom the best that could be found elsewhere of insight and wisdom and reflexion on experience and soaring speculation and transcendence of the finite—the best of all there had been of seeing the infinite in and through the finite— seems to belong by native right, so that it is all His own, and it flows from Him spontaneously whatever the special problem, or occupation, or situation at the moment may be. It is just the natural expression of Himself. We have the sense that He lived sanely and

securely in this sphere or on this plane; that though
He belonged to His own age in His ways of picturing
reality, and had no share in what is called modern
knowledge, and stood aloof even from the practical
activities of His own time and some of the permanent
concerns and interests and deepest affections of normal
life in the world as it was and is; yet in all these matters,
too, if we could have His mind, His spirit, directed to
them, there is no guidance we could trust as we could
trust His.

This, I believe, is our main reason for believing in
Him—the experience of life itself; and the reason
grows stronger as that experience grows longer, so
that we know a man's life has worth in the measure in
which we can write as his epitaph 'He was beginning
to be a disciple of Jesus', whether he knew it or not.

The validity of this reason for belief in Jesus Christ
is in no way impaired by our knowledge that we
cannot trust as historical in the narrower sense of the
word the details of the picture of His life given us in
our Gospels. Those who are familiar with the work of
the last fifty years on the Gospels are for the most part
agreed that real historical memories underlie them,
and that they contain much real history and faithful
record of teaching and incident. There is neither
deliberate falsification nor conscious idealization. But
we know how inevitably the personal element enters
into statements of experience, and the presuppositions
of those who are the subjects of the experience determine the account of it they give. And, besides, it is
agreed that none of the Gospels as we have them took
form till the new Religion had been many years in

being and Christians and local Churches wanted coherent accounts of the origin of their religion for their own edification or for others to read who wanted, or ought, to be informed. So there is no argument and no reasoning that can prevail against the view, which is widely current today among Christians, that some of our narratives, which have been regarded as plain records of actual incidents, belong not to the prosaic plane of history but to the poetry of Faith. If poetry is too vague a term, more exact expressions are to hand, ugly as they are—the aetiology or the aretology of already existing religious belief. Why do we feel towards Jesus as we do? How could He be what we believe He is? Or again, He is our Lord, the Son of GOD: let us praise and magnify Him as we ought. Some of our narratives are answers to these questions or expressions of this religious instinct. They shew us vividly the profound impression produced by the experience of which Jesus was the immediate subject, as He was also the centre of similar experience for some of His contemporaries and earliest followers. They shew us the conditions in which the new religion sprang up and the Christian Church came into being. It is real life in which it had its origin, and when we understand that it is a picture-book rather than a history in which some of the features of this experience are described, we can form a more intimate appreciation of it and the better enter into it ourselves, if we will, and relate it more surely to our own conditions.

Nor, again, is such a belief as I have indicated dependent on the theological system which was gradually built up on the basis of traditional beliefs and customs, and the *data* of gospels and epistles invested, from the time when the collection was made, with infallible authority as transmitting both true history in detail and true interpretation of its significance.

We cannot grant the premisses. Infallibilities of all kinds are gone. Many a presupposition about GOD and the world and Man that was pre-Christian enters into the scheme, and was not Christianized by being made part of the structure of the doctrine of the Church. To many students of it today the outstanding characteristic of this theological system as a whole is the fact that the central Christian conviction, that Jesus Christ, the Man-GOD and GOD-Man, was the revelation of reality, was not allowed free course in it.

I am not proposing to ask you to follow up in detail this line of thought today, or to weigh the value of our theological system in the past. We know that the whole system needs re-basing and re-interpreting in relation to convictions, intellectual and ethical, that guide the best life and thought of our time. So it is not to our traditional theological system that we look for reasons for our belief in Jesus Christ today. But the fact that it must be in our minds leads me to what seems to me to be as sure a ground of belief as the one we have considered.

Our whole attitude to Jesus today would be gravely affected if knowledge that has accrued, especially in recent years, did not justify belief in Him as Incarnate Son of GOD, very Man of very Man, very GOD of very GOD. I pause for a moment to emphasize the fact that Christian Faith is in One who was at once both very Man of very Man and very GOD of very GOD. It is as heretical not to believe that reality in its aspect of manhood was manifest in Him as not to believe that reality in its aspect of godhead was manifest in Him. No alternations of personality were allowed in the formal doctrine of the Church: He was one, and the One was human and divine. The tradition of the historical experience was strong enough to maintain itself so far. But its implications as regards Man's true relation to GOD were so remote from common experience and the ideas of the various religiosities and philosophies of the times during which Christian doctrines were in the making, that the duality excluded by the fundamental Christian conviction permeates the whole ecclesiastical system. It is only this fundamental Christian conviction that our enquiry this morning has in view. In the light of modern knowledge, how can we regard Jesus in His personal life and being as revealing to us, not just here Man as he really is, and there GOD, but steadily and continuously the truth of GOD and Man? I can only attempt to indicate the answer which I am sure is in the minds of many here—the answer which many more have discerned and are waiting to hear, not from free-lances or groups in the Church, but from the Church itself.

There has come to our own age, mainly in my own lifetime, and largely through the patient labours and insight of truth-loving men of our own race, a revelation of Truth which as surely marks a new era in the history of human progress as did the emergence of Jesus. Though it may be long before all the implications of it are worked out, the vital truth, of which the term 'Evolution' is perhaps an inconvenient symbol rather than the best expression, is established. Defence of the Christian Religion which does not recognize this truth will not serve the Church of the future. What is needed is a gospel wholly permeated by it, in its history, its philosophy, its ethics—its whole theology, which will also be its anthropology and its eschatology. In the new perspective in which we see the facts of life, does Jesus Christ still hold His central place?

What the new revelation shews us is that the world and everything in it, including Man, have come to be what they are in virtue of inherent powers and capacities, by processes that have been continuous and orderly through time, in computing which a thousand years is only as it were a unit. The highest resultant of the process, so far as we know, is Man, who alone is able, in some measure, to transcend and, as concerns himself at least, to direct the process. The evolutionary process is still going on, and what Man may become can only be imagined. He is clearly not yet so perfectly adapted to his environment, nor so mastered by it, nor so specialized, that further progress is precluded.

I have used the word 'progress'. A wrong use may have been made in the past of the idea of Progress and the indefinite perfectibility of Man. Recent protests against it may be as salutary as they have been piquant. But the fact is established that the chart of Man's history, if it shews him pursuing blind alleys at times, and, with all the odds apparently against him, learning his way very slowly, with leaps and misses and long periods of stagnation (and this is just what I under-

stand our biologists find in their studies in lower organic
life); and if this chart of Man's history shews him never
making progress except by struggle and suffering; yet
it shews a sustained and persistent rise in the scale of
life from the time when the variation occurred and the
human being was differentiated from the common
stock of man and ape. If our charts are large enough,
we see that, although the lines which have risen high
may drop or vanish altogether, always other lines begin
to rise. Taking the history of the race as a whole, it
shews persistency of effort, recuperation, and renewal
as an inherent characteristic of Man. If our present
civilization should indeed prove to be some such blind
alley as those in which men lost themselves in the past,
yet all the evidence available suggests that thousands
of years hence some other civilization higher than our
own will have arisen in its place. And this persistent
urge in the race as a whole, through failure after
failure; this striving after a good, the nature of which
is imperfectly understood; this character of Man,
which belongs to his very constitution and is as much
his own as his body is his own, is best interpreted—for
it is persons who are concerned—in terms of an eternal
purpose informing and guiding the race to its highest
good while never violating the inherent moral in-
dependence of free personality. In the moral world of
persons there is no room for Omnipotence as irre-
sistible force, nor any way but the ·way of free co-
operation.[1]

Purpose in detail it is often beyond us to discern.
Mr Hardy's fascinating picture of the unconscious will

[1] See on this point, e.g. Dr Oman's *Grace and Personality*.

of the universe, with its logical contradiction, is drawn
in the light of experience. But we have to look from
the chaos of atoms to the cosmos, from the amoeba to
primitive man, from primitive man to the highest man
who has yet come to be. And then, though the end
may still be hidden from us, what we know of the past
suggests that there is an end, a purpose to 'fashion all
things fair' through men and their failures, and that
it is in men themselves that the consciousness is dim
and the will weak. They could adapt themselves to it
and be its expression if they would, for they are already
its partial expression. We believe in Jesus Christ because He is to us the type of the perfect adaptation
and expression.

I have to write this paper independently of the one
we shall have heard on the question *Why we believe in
God*. I assume that the conception of purpose will have
figured in it, and the corollary that where purpose can
be detected personal activity is implied. To recognize
an eternal purpose in Man and his history is to see a
Divine activity operating in him and a Divine end to
be achieved not only in him but through him: so that
he is the impersonation of the purpose, which lives in
him and works through him, slowly adapting to the
end in view, stage by stage, everything in him that
does not serve it.

If we left GOD out of account, we should have no
clue to the meaning of the facts of the universe and
life as we know them now. With that hypothesis and
the idea of Incarnation to guide us, they become coherent. Intelligence answers intelligence. Deep calls
to deep, and deep responds. The whole world is in-

carnation in process: in man it becomes increasingly personal: and in the course of the process, 'in the fullness of the times', in Jesus Christ the manifestation of GOD in Humanity reached its highest stage.

So with the evidence of the evolution of the world and Man to guide us, we are led, no less surely than our forefathers were led, to belief in Jesus Christ, which we can express in their terms though many of our presuppositions are different from theirs. It seems clear to me that St John in his doctrine of the Logos and the Spirit, and in such a saying as 'My Father worketh hitherto and I work', and St Paul with his idea of eternal purpose and the patience of GOD and the Christ in whom and through whom and unto whom all things were created, the Christ who is in process of 'being fulfilled', were pointing to the truth of Evolution that has come to us.

If it be felt that this kind of belief in the Incarnate Son of GOD, who emerges in the process of human history and enters human life as the manifestation of the truth of Humanity, to be the *Christus Consummator*, the Type, the Example, the Inspiration of Mankind, is belief in a Jesus Christ 'from below', and not in the Son of GOD who 'came down from heaven', we must insist that it is not so to anyone who sees GOD in the process all through. Anyone who still holds to the dichotomies of Man and GOD, the natural and the supernatural, discovery and revelation, and the like, and does not see that the Christian doctrine of the Incarnation implies that the process of human life is at once and inseparably both human and divine, at once both 'from below' and 'from above', and that it can never reach its goal till the divine is fully expressed in the human, must be left to the old orthodoxies and infallibilities which guided our forefathers to noble lives.

Meanwhile, the fact that after 1900 years we are beginning to understand that ruin threatens our 'Christian' civilization unless we can strengthen and develop the Christian factors in it, and that now for the first time in human history the ideal scheme of life that Jesus sketched is beginning to win its way on its intrinsic merits, confirms, I think, the main argument of this paper. The ideal of the Kingdom of GOD on earth, at once personal and social, is envisaged, no doubt, much more as 'the relief of man's estate' than as 'the glory of GOD'. Jesus Himself may be far less regarded today as the Saviour of mankind, because none of the doctrines of Fall of Man and Atonement and Heaven and Hell, which are generally known as Christian, are credible today. But His ideas and ideals as to the relations that ought to exist between man and man as a condition of human society are becoming socially effective as they never were while those doctrines reigned and the world was regarded as a perishing world disfigured by Man, rather than as GOD's world, potentially and progressively, but only through Man's free co-operation, His perfect organ—the end to be as much Man's achievement as GOD's.

§ VIII

THE CHRISTIAN DOCTRINE OF MAN[1]

We are GOD's fellow-workers.	1 Cor. iii. 9.
Fellow-workers with the truth.	3 John 8.
The glorious liberty of the children of GOD.	Rom. viii. 21.

I want to speak today of the Christian doctrine of Man and to invite the Churchmen's Union to a new crusade to rescue it from the *débris* of Jewish and pagan conceptions by which from the very beginning it has been obscured.

But first, as I am not a member of your Union, though in close fellowship of the spirit with you, I want to express the profound gratitude that is due to your Union for the services it has rendered to the truth. You are the only Church Society that puts truth in the forefront of its programme. You put it above 'old custom', old tradition, old beliefs. You obviously trust in the immortal promise that the Spirit of Christ, which is the Spirit of His Father—the very Spirit of Truth—shall guide His disciples—all who will learn of Him—age after age along the way of truth. And while you believe that the eternal Logos of GOD, which is the light that has always lighted every man, was supremely manifest in Christ; you do not think that this birth-privilege of men was lost from the moment when He came into the world, nor do you claim—as the Church has seemed to claim—a monopoly of

[1] A Sermon preached in St Andrew's Church, Westminster, on 27 May 1924, at the Corporate Celebration of the Holy Communion of the Churchmen's Union.

divine enlightenment ever after for the organized Society of Christians. The Incarnation, you are sure, did not limit the activities of the Spirit of GOD to the narrow confines of the Church. So wherever new knowledge comes, in every department of human experience and activity, you are ready to welcome it as the gift of the Spirit of Truth, and to revise every belief and every judgement of the past that is in any way discordant with the new knowledge that is at once both 'given' and 'won'. And this you do knowing what it is you do, with a loyalty that passes the understanding of many who are loyal in other ways to Him who called Himself, as Tertullian said, 'not ancient custom, but Truth'.

And you can do it—how strange it is that it needs to be said!—you can do it within the Church of England. Ecclesiastical authorities whose business it is to keep things as they are may cold-shoulder you; the pulpits of the land may ring for a season with denunciations of you, for alas! the people who know better are seldom found in congregations to cry 'shame!' You might almost think you were living where the writ of the Vatican Council ran.

Historical memories are short. Let me recall the decree of the Vatican Council of some fifty years ago:

If anyone shall say that it is possible, that from time to time in the course of the progress of science an interpretation may have to be attributed to dogmas proposed by the Church other than that which has been and is understood by the Church: let him be accursed.

There speaks the authentic voice of Rome. So Rome must speak when the Vatican Council meets again next year.

But it is not the voice of England. An English bishop may write in *The Times* and say we have many doctrines in common with Rome, and must not raise again the 'No Popery' cry. But it is certain that in one form or other that cry will always be raised in England when changes in our Services are proposed that would re-introduce or suggest and encourage a doctrine that was rejected at the Reformation, not because it was Roman, but because it was untrue.

It was not for nothing that the fires of Smithfield burnt. And Latimer's words to Ridley, 'We shall this day light such a candle, by God's grace, in England as I trust shall never be put out', express, I am convinced, the mind of England as truly today as they did at that dark moment in our history when they were uttered. The spirit of reformation has ever since had its home in the Church of England, the spirit that is sensitive to new learning and new conditions and ever finding those new interpretations of 'dogmas proposed by the Church' that the Vatican abhors.

From time to time we have our crises. There was one ten years ago, when a sudden attack was made on 'the critical school', the students and scholars who can never be counted in more than tens. Thousands were marshalled against them. The Churchmen's Union played its part, and the freedom needed at the moment was securely won: freedom to investigate the origins and history of our religion, freedom to question traditional views and ignore the literal sense of old beliefs and formulas and affirm them in their meaning for religion today; freedom to speak out and, in the name of the Christian religion, repudiate ideas that the Church had held as the framework of its faith, when those ideas have become irrational and immoral. I say 'become' irrational and immoral, because in my judgement those terms are always relative. They always have in view a standard, and in these matters the standard must be the best knowledge and the highest ethical sense of any particular age; and judged by the standards of today, alike in knowledge of the universe and the story of Man's emergence and place in it (learned as it were but yesterday) and in far finer sensitiveness to the ethical ideals of Christ and their bearing on human life both individual and social, there is much in our traditional conceptions of GOD and Man that is irrational and immoral.

We cannot expect our presentation of the truth to be free from the myth and imagery and picture-thinking and all the analogies drawn from the very experience out of which the truth has been reached. These myths and pictures are still, I suppose always will be, for many the nearest representation of the truth. But we cannot ask less than Plato demanded for the youth of his Republic: that ancient myths which suggest unworthy ideas of GOD should be discarded and those only retained which are *like* the truth. Dr J. M. Wilson, one of your veterans, has just been pleading for reforms on these lines in our religious teaching of the young; and they are long overdue. Many apologists of late have set their hands to restatement of the Christian doctrine of GOD, but nearly always I seem to see the old ideas dressed up again: and I believe another way of approach must be tried. I despair of reaching a true doctrine of GOD along the

130

lines that the Church has followed in its traditional system of dogma. Orthodox Christology blocks the way, with its dichotomy of the human and the divine in the very Person in whom we believe they were manifestly one. We have not yet learned the meaning of the Incarnation, which is our central belief.

Dr Gore, one of the noblest and most persuasive exponents of some convictions that all Christians share, and the most competent apologist of lost theological causes that I know, in reviewing Dr Raven's *Apollinarianism* insists that the distinctness of nature between Godhead and manhood is 'the basis which our Lord's language about GOD and man assumes'; and with the same intention he writes of 'the foundation of Israel on which the Church is built'; as if the Church of Christ, the Israel of GOD, was pledged to the Jewish conception of GOD. I do not like Dr Gore's inanimate metaphors with all the fixity they imply, when we are dealing with living human hearts and minds and the religious interpretation of live human experience. They do not correspond with anything we know of the processes of life and personality in any of its manifestations and expressions which we can observe.

No doubt 'the man Jesus' had the roots of His being far back in his remotest ancestor. His ideas of GOD had nearer roots in some of the prophets and psalmists of Israel. He was, of course, the product of the past. But like all other children born into the world, He was something new, different from all others that had ever been or would be; and from the moment of His birth He was drawing in from His whole environment, acting on it and reacting to it. His experience was His very own; and the outcome of that experience, as He told it and shewed it, was a new doctrine of GOD and Man. It was not the old Jewish doctrine. It was a new growth. Our metaphors must not be architectural, but biological, and only *epigenesis* will describe the facts. It is a case not of adding a coping-stone to a venerable pile, nor of mere evolution, but of the emergence out of new experience of something gloriously new, creature and creator.

I cannot think that Dr Gore is right. The Jews of the Fourth Gospel, whether they were our Lord's contemporaries or of the next generation, had, I believe, a truer appreciation of the facts. Marcion may have gone too far, or St Paul not far enough. It may be a question whether our Lord Himself quite understood or gave full expression to the content and implications of His experience, or whether His reporters fell short in their reports. But this is certain. The horror of 'the Jews' at His calling GOD His Father in a really personal sense (for that is how we should render the words in English today) shews plainly that they understood His conception of GOD and Man to be radically different from their own.

It is just here that the contribution He brought to the religious interpretation of life has all the newness, the 'otherness' if you like, that makes it a 'revelation' —first of all, as in His great Thanksgiving (Mt. xi. 25 ff. and Lk. x. 21 f.) He tells us it was, to Himself, and then through Him to us. And I can attach no meaning to this metaphor, this human analogy, of the Fatherhood of GOD; this personal Fatherhood and Sonship, 'my

Father and your Father', 'Father', the new name
which men are to use of GOD; unless it connotes, not
distinctness, but community of nature between Godhead and manhood. And if the Jews of the Fourth
Gospel could not believe it at all, and the Church has
built up a stately edifice of doctrine on 'the foundation of Israel', yet in prayer and sacrament it has
surpassed its creed and left ways open by which, in
defiance of dogma, men might for the moment bridge
the pre-supposed chasm of nature between themselves and GOD.

We commonly speak of the doctrine of the Incarnation as our interpretation of the *Person* of our Lord.
We should do better to say of His *experience*, and to go
further still and add the experience of others who were
brought into contact with Him—the personal experience of which He was the subject and the much wider
experience of which He was the creator and the centre.

Our exploitation of this doctrine in the past has
been far too one-sided. We have not had the courage
of our conviction that in this experience we have a true
revelation of the relation existing not only between the
man Jesus and GOD, but *therefore* from the beginning
between all men and GOD. The experience of Jesus
answered all the old logicians' questions, *An sit, quid
sit, quale sit*. The doctrinal system of the Church denied
that the answers were true of Man as Man. It has
Judaized, and Platonized, and Stoicized, and Aristo-
telized in turn; and now willy-nilly it must Evolu-
tionize. And the wonder is that when it does this it
begins to Christianize, and the alienated world of
today will listen again to the Church when it sets

before it this doctrine of Man implicit in the experience of Jesus.

For all that we know today of the constitution of the universe, of the whole realm of Nature, of the processes that have been and are in operation, of all the history of the world and Man, obliges us either to leave GOD out of account, or else to see Him in the whole evolutionary process, with Man as fellow-worker with Him and the higher stages of the process, which begin with man's appearance on the scene, as much dependent on Man as on GOD. 'We are GOD's fellow-workers'—we are partners with Him in the whole business of life, in the whole process of the world.

Some years ago we were urged to give up our phrase 'Incarnation' as a pagan conception. But that is not our way. Phrases, ideograms, are not like wine-skins. More and more with growing knowledge we fill our Christian ideograms with new content and they bear the pressure, and again and again we find that an old 'formula' has a far wider application and a deeper verification than those who used it in the past could know. We talk less glibly of 'dead' matter than our fathers did. And more and more I am sure it will be found that 'Incarnation' is the term that best expresses for us the truth about the world and Man. It is all Incarnation: a process, from the beginning, if beginning there was, to the end, if end there be. But I am keeping you too long.

My appeal to you is this. In the past the Church has limited its doctrine of Incarnation to its interpretation of one historical experience, an experience which marked the culmination of one stage in the evolution of Man and the beginning of a new era. For Jesus was the Supreme Idealist, and wherever His Spirit has had free course it has been impossible for anyone to think of GOD or of Man or of human society as men thought before. The Church has been the guardian of a great Revelation, but it has used it almost exclusively for its doctrine of GOD. Yet the one certain fact is that Jesus was a man, and of course the doctrine of the Church has preserved this fact. But it has never yet used it in its doctrine of Man. It has isolated 'the man Jesus' from His place in the historic evolutionary process. 'My Father worketh hitherto and I work.' Oh, there is evidence enough of other interpretations before we entered the prison house of Latinized and world-denying Christianity.

It is irrational today to use your Incarnation only for your doctrine of GOD, and not for your doctrine of Man. The GOD-Man is a revelation of Everyman as well as of GOD, and your doctrine of Everyman must be derived from what He was.

So my appeal to the Churchmen's Union is to put in the forefront of its programme the attempt to state for the first time a doctrine of Man consistent—I may not say with the Church's doctrine of the Incarnation, but with the conviction that the truth about Man is disclosed in Jesus Christ no less than the truth about GOD. So at last we may have a 'Christian' doctrine of Man by which Man today may be 'saved'.

OUR TRADITIONAL FORMULARIES[1]

The prevalent dissatisfaction with our existing formularies is many-sided. Some of our most Christianly-minded friends would have none of them. Others would wish to eliminate everything metaphysical from their creed and substitute for it statements of ethical principle and aspiration. Others again are mainly affected by particular clauses or phrases which affirm or imply beliefs, historical, ethical, scientific, which they have come to regard as misleading or even positively untrue. There were not many of us, I suppose, who had to wait for Dr Otto's fine book to learn that religion in its distinctive character is neither moral nor rational. If scrutiny of ourselves was not sufficiently illuminating, we had only to look round among our religious friends in order to discover how much remained even in the Christian religion of primitive conceptions neither moralized nor rationalized. But one of the great merits of Dr Otto's book which has not, I think, been sufficiently recognized—other attractions have obscured it—is that he shews the gradual emergence in religion of the moral and the rational. The mark of the great religion is not its success in maintaining the primitive sense of the 'numinous'.[2]

---

[1] A paper read at the Conference of Modern Churchmen held at Selly Oak, August 1927.

[2] I keep Dr Otto's word for the 'sacred' or the 'holy'—the element of 'other'-ness in man's experience of the universe and life, consciousness of which is the ground and the matter of religion.

It would cease to be a religion if it did not keep this sense alive. But it shews its greatness by the measure in which it is able to direct this sense to moral and rational ends, and in its conception of the 'numinous' at least keep pace with the ethical and intellectual evolution of a progressive race and its civilization. In this essential and critical function of a great religion it is bound to find its sacred books and formularies of all kinds an impediment and a drag.

This is our experience today. Jesus in His world-view, His attitude to life and His teaching, His valuation of reality, working on the religious conceptions of His time, both moralized and rationalized those conceptions to the highest degree. It is always to His conception of the Father-God and His ethical ideals that we turn. The Church by its valuation of Him, its estimate of the significance of His experience and of His place in the whole order of reality, which the doctrine of the Incarnation, rightly understood, implies, established for ever, as we believe, the standard of measure of truth. The Church has had in its hands ever since the master-key to the understanding of the scheme of things.

It used it effectively in its early solutions of the moral and intellectual problems by which it was confronted. But different conditions and different problems need different solutions. And the formularies of all kinds which embody the solutions that were adequate to the moral and intellectual conditions of the past are in some respects below the level of the demands of ethics and reason today. We have new keys to knowledge and moral judgement in our hands in all the new learning about the world and Man and the fascinating story of the drama of their evolution. Wherever these things are concerned, our formularies represent an older learning, not always the best of its time, which nowadays discredits the religion of which they are supposed to be, so far as they go, the expression. Yet when we use the master-key of the doctrine of the Incarnation we find that it fits all the new knowledge and experience of our time, and opens out to us an interpretation of the world, a revelation of God and His purpose and way of working, and a revelation of Man, which at once satisfies and stimulates our intellectual cravings and our moral sense. Our religion is the Incarnation, the God-Man, the Cross the way of Life, the ever-emerging, insuppressible, conquering Good. Our religion ought not even to seem to harbour bits of obsolete history, ethics, and science. That, I suppose, should be one of our guiding principles of revision.

Dr Major has already given us an introduction to our discussion this evening. In his article in the July number of *The Modern Churchman* he has depicted the position as it presents itself, I suppose, to most of us in general and in respect of various details. In this article he says: 'Today traditional Christianity with its scheme of salvation lies shattered: it has lost intellectual authority with all classes'; and he quotes Mrs Humphry Ward's description of Modernism as 'the attempt of the modern spirit, acting religiously, to refashion Christianity, not outside, but inside the warm limits of the ancient churches, to secure not a reduced, but a transformed Christianity'.

I presuppose that general statement and that description. In Dr Major's statement, as I understand
it, the stress lies on the words 'its scheme of salvation'.
I should wish to add to his statement my own conviction that our traditional Christianity has to a large
extent lost moral authority also, because of its obsolete
anthropology; but I cannot enlarge on that part of the
subject now. I must, however, adopt for myself a
limitation which Dr Major seems to reject when he
criticises Mrs Ward's expression 'the ancient churches'.
No doubt the need is the same in all the churches of
more recent origin that have formularies at all; but
it is inside one of the ancient churches, sharing its life
to the full, and within its order, that we ourselves have
to work.

I hope I shall not be wasting your time if I dwell a
moment on this point as marking for us at once a
principle and a limitation. None of us, I am sure,
harbours any idea of a new church or a new religion.
We know that in the past Christianity and the Church
have passed through many stages of the process of
change and developement that the world and everything in it exhibits, and our chief concern at the
moment is that this natural change and developement
should have free play in our own Church. We do not
want it to be artificially arrested through the false
idea, as we hold it, that the only way of safeguarding
the sense of the numinous in its specific Christian
manifestation is by the revival of beliefs and practices
of times before the Reformation. In all ages the
'modern' churchmen have been those who responded
more easily than others to the stimulus of new thought

and knowledge, new ideas and experience, new revelations of the spirit of Man and of GOD, and sought to
domesticate them all in the Church and the religion
it offered men as their guide to the truth of things in
life and thought. If Christianity began with Christ, it
was certainly refashioned by St Paul, by St John, by
a long series of thinkers and teachers, Fathers and
Doctors and Councils, after them. The sixteenth
century witnessed refashioning of a more obvious kind
on a large scale and in a great part of Western
Christendom, and the ancient Church of England was
refashioned by the march of events and the peculiar
genius of the English people in such strange wise as
to preserve its continuity, and retain all the characteristic features of historical Christianity, while adapting in various ways its constitution and teaching to the
new conditions and ideas of the time. So, having lived
as it seems almost from hand to mouth for more than
a hundred years, it found itself established in the
unique position in Christendom that it has occupied
since and occupies today. Catholic and Protestant,
primitive, mediaeval, and reformed, respecting an-
tiquity and all that we call 'tradition'; but not
inaccessible to fresh knowledge and new movements;
tenacious of the faith once delivered to the saints, but
claiming no infallibility for the interpretations even
of the most august assemblies of the faithful in the
past. 'General Councils may err, and sometimes have
erred, even in things pertaining unto God' (*Article* xxi).
By its history in the past, by the very personality and
character its special experience have developed in it,
it seems to be marked out as the destined representa-

tive of an organic Christianity continuously developing and shaping itself anew to meet the constantly changing conditions of knowledge and thought and life that determine for men the real world, generation after generation, that confronts them.

I wish that what Bishop Creighton and other historians in the Victorian era wrote about it, and Mr Fawkes's little book of only a few years ago, could be broadcasted for the use of our official representatives today. The Church of England is so splendidly worth saving in its unique historical character. Whoever else goes out of the Church of England, Modernists must not; for it is their natural home, and true appreciation of its character seems to be in danger of being left to them. So in all essays in reinterpretation and reformulation let us cherish the consciousness that we are first and foremost and all the time concerned with the Church of England. It is in and through the Church of England that the new presentation of Christianity must be made, if the religion of the future is not to sweep away all ancient landmarks and institutions. And we must remember that we can only save by serving.

If we accept this principle, the limitation it imposes on us is severe. For many of our natural allies are but sleeping members of the Church, and by its new constitution have no power to influence its future: and the modern moralizing and rationalizing of traditional Christianity has progressed in recent years too fast for the rank and file of English Churchmen to keep pace with it, and it does not yet seem to them to be what it has been to those engaged in it—a spiritualizing process which liberates the spirit of Man only by bringing

him into closer immediate communion with the spirit
of Christ.

How then is the needed evolution to be expedited?
Is it to be by reformulation of ancient formularies?
To be sure there is precedent for this course. We know
that it was reformulation that gave us our Book of
Common Prayer and our Articles of Religion. There
was no new knowledge then of the facts of the beginnings of Christianity: no new knowledge of the primitive
background, lacking which the new authority given
to the Bible was a snare. There was no new science:
the earth was still the centre of the universe with the
sun as its satellite. But there was a new learning, and
a quickened sense of spiritual and moral values in
religion, and on the whole the reformulation carried
out by the Church of England was a fine achievement
of the Modernism of the sixteenth century—typically
English.

Can we hope for as good results from reformulation
today? The attempt has been made. Unlike many
who are here tonight, I am one of those who have had
no share in making it. Apart from joining in the plea
that, whatever was done, we should have one Order
for Holy Communion as the use of the undivided
Church of England, I have been only a spectator of
other men's work; and now I only attempt to estimate
the result in its bearings on the question before us this
evening. I have no information about the proceedings
of the Archbishops' Committee on Doctrine, which
might be instructive, so I can take only the instance
of the Prayer Book—the most obvious firstfruits of the
new constitution of the Church of England.

'All was in confusion; Nous came and brought order.' In this case Nous 'in commission', distributed in uncertain proportions between vicar, church council, and bishop, is to establish the order, congregation by congregation. It seems to me that we are to have a period of sanctioned confusion in the form of permissible variations. As a mirror of the state of the Church of England today, the new book reveals the absence of controlling mind, common will and consciousness—a position of instability. Anyone can fish in these troubled waters. But that is not why the Churchmen's Union has given its official blessing to the book. It is, I infer, because of some new freedoms, modernizations of words, additional prayers, omissions or attenuations of phrases that obtrude ideas once as firmly believed as they are today generally rejected, all of which changes indicate movement to something better than was. Here and there, I think, they imply a modification of traditional doctrine in the same direction.

As regards the new Order for Holy Communion, we are assured that no change of doctrine is meant or intended. Yet the new Order will have in future the same authority as the old one. Where the teaching of the Church of England is in question the old Order will have to be interpreted by the new one. It will be a question of the legal construction of the two documents, the older in the light of the newer; and I cannot but believe that doctrine deliberately rejected at the Reformation, because it was neither moral nor rational, now becomes inferentially permissible, and therefore sanctioned as it was not before.

143

If a case like that of the baptismal regeneration controversy, *mutatis mutandis*, was before such a body as
the Judicial Committee of the Privy Council, I think
they would certainly infer such doctrine as the *rationale*
of the new order. In this instance, if I am right,
reformulation points backwards. It takes us back to
a lower moral and rational level than we were on
before.

But more instructive still for our purpose is an instance to which special attention is due, for it exhibits
definitely doctrinal reformulation—the new Order for
the Baptism of Infants. There are changes which
nearly everyone will welcome. But, but! The old
Order contains a highly technical term which has been
the subject of much controversy: 'seeing now...that
this child is regenerate'. Various interpretations of
this term have been given and allowed in the Church
of England as expressing the effects of baptism. It has
become, as it were, a blank cheque on which you can
write values in your own coinage. It is replaced by
the good plain English 'born again'. True, 'born
again' stands in the Authorized Version of the Nicodemus episode in the Fourth Gospel (Jn. iii). But it
was corrected to 'anew', or 'from above', in the
Revised Version, and even in our Order of 1662 it
stands as 'born anew'. It was only Nicodemus who
thought it must mean being born a second time, and
we ourselves only use the phrase 'twice-born' of adults
who have had some conscious experience, which is
impossible in infants. To assert it as the result of the
baptism of an infant, to say in plain English that this
is what Baptism does, is to take back from us the

freedom of interpretation of a technical term that had been won in the process of moralizing our traditional doctrine of sacraments. And it is extraordinarily hard to devise an ethical *rationale* of the sacrament of Baptism in the case of infants. This is the only instance of outspoken reformulation that has caught my eye, and in it Modernism loses heavily by the change—as I imagine its opponents must have realized with some amusement, if membership of such learned assemblies does not atrophy the sense of humour.

So I am led, by this evidence of the results of the laborious and prayerful work of good and learned men today, to the conclusion that the Church of England as a whole is not ready for reformulation of doctrine. Let us have no attempts at present at formal replacements by anything like official authority of the technical terms of traditional Christianity. It is not in that way that the refashioning we want can be done.

Let us not seek to find other terms for Incarnation, Sin, Forgiveness, Atonement, Resurrection, Salvation, Eternal Life, Communion of Saints, Heaven and Hell, or any of our technical terms. Let us rather go on as we have been doing, interpreting, explaining, openly repudiating some meanings which in the past have been connected with particular terms and expressions, treating them all as provisional and contingent, but keeping them as part of the common stock of our religious language.

If need be, we justify them in general, as we generally can, in relation to the particular environment of which they were the product. But as regards the present we take them one by one and fill them out with meanings that correspond to the knowledge and experience of today. We treat them as symbols of the realities which from the beginning they were devised to reflect and represent—realities of which our conceptions are different from those which have been prevalent in the past and are still in backward popular belief attached to the terms. We commend our interpretations, our revaluations of old beliefs, to the *communis sensus fidelium* and seek its sanction. I have no doubt that in time that sanction will be given.

Far more generally than even ten years ago men and women, having ceased to treat the Bible as a store-house of information about God and the World and Man, have come to regard it rather, New Testament as well as Old, as a picture-book of Religion, in which the religious experience pourtrayed is the revealed and revealing fact, and the description of it only a picture of the fact in the fashion of the time.

We have to treat our doctrines as the product of picture-thinking of a similar kind, pictorial representations of religious realities, and seek to construct pictures in the fashion of our own times. That method will give us, not the legal, but the religious, construction of our formularies. I have no doubt that Dr J. M. Wilson is moved by the true prophetic spirit—the spirit that discerns and speaks out the things of God—when he pleads and urges that the picture for our own times must be dominated by the evolutionist conception of the world and life. That will give us beyond question a transformed Christianity. We shall keep those of our legends and pictures which are suggestive of what is true, to stimulate our children's and refresh our own imagination. We shall keep them in our richly furnished Church of England for those who are still at the level of thought and belief to which they correspond. In the course of our revaluation of old beliefs we shall be content with fewer affirmations and we shall leave many questions open.

Will our valuation, therefore, be less Christian? Will it be a 'reduced' Christianity that results? I am not sure what the phrase means, but we know that this group of Churchmen are always charged with being 'humanistic' and 'Unitarian' in their views. There is never a Conference of this kind that is not followed by criticism to that effect. What are the facts? Shall we be 'humanistic' in our religion?

Certainly the refashioned evolutionist Christianity will set a higher value on the World and Man than traditional Christianity has ever allowed them. It will treat disparagement of either not as pious, but as positively irreligious. It will glory in the long travail and the achievements of the spirit of Man. In this way it will be frankly humanist. The World and Man will receive at last the valuation that is implied in the doctrine of the Incarnation.

But will GOD, therefore, have less place in it? Will there be less recognition of the GOD in Christ reconciling the world to Himself? A man is religious, I suppose, in proportion as he is conscious of GOD and brings that consciousness to bear on his conception and conduct of life; and the characteristic note of Christian religion is the particular variety of that consciousness that results from the conviction that Jesus in His whole experience was the manifestation of GOD in flesh—the

147

hidden GOD in the World and Man, thus for the first time clearly revealed.

And what are the facts as to the second charge? Shall we be 'Unitarian' in our religion?

Well, it must be said quite plainly that our critics do not seem to know that the old Unitarianism is dead. To the Unitarian the principle that GOD is one, as an entity self-contained and exclusive of all else, was fundamental. Over against Him was set the Universe and Man. The antithesis, GOD and Man, was ultimate. Therefore of no man could godhead be predicated.

The evolutionist Christianity, on the contrary, does not attempt to conceive of GOD apart from the Universe (that question belongs to the realm of pure speculation) or in antithesis to Man. Its faith is fixed on GOD as the ground of all being and creative activity, manifested in the Universe, and in Man, however partially, yet more fully than in aught else. In every man by his very nature and constitution there is a faint image of godhead. In Jesus—His personality and character and life—there was a full image, and so in Him we bow down before and worship godhead in its most visible human embodiment. 'No man hath seen God at any time'. Here, in Jesus, is the most revealing vision.

To a Unitarian the doctrine of the Trinity is a piece of incredible metaphysics. To us it is a picture of the reality of the life and activity of GOD. Father and Son are of course purely human similes; but just because the Modernist believes that all that is is grounded in GOD, he is not frightened by human analogies; and, believing that the experiences of human life in the

148

world in their fundamental character are not unlike but (on however lower a plane) like the experience of GOD, he readily pictures the Divine Life and activity in terms of Father, Son, and Spirit. He conceives of the Divine Life as one of eternal self-communication, outgoing, giving. He does not fear anthropomorphisms just because he believes that the whole process of the world is a manifestation of GOD, and that in the highest human capacities and relationships He is most clearly revealed.

So the Christianity that is refashioned by the evolutionist knowledge of today will be bold to proclaim the old gospel of the doctrines of the Incarnation and the Kingdom of GOD, and the Future Coming of the Christ in glory, as the meaning of the whole process and the true picture of Man's significance and place in the scheme of things, and so of his responsibility as a free agent to further the process. For it is an account of ourselves that we give, an account of every man, when we affirm our faith in the man Jesus as incarnate Son of GOD. And on evolutionist lines we say there is plan discernible and purpose. There is a trend to good: good has emerged; against all odds, as it might seem, it has been produced. Man as we know him at his best is the latest and highest order of being evolved: all else has gone to the making of him, and he includes elements of all else. High moral personality is not a by-product of the process but the outcome of its travail.

We cannot define this 'personality'. But we know it by its manifestations, and personality which is the outcome of the process must serve us as an index to the characteristic quality of the creative principle of all. A directing spirit is the image by which we picture it most truly: not 'impersonal'; it cannot lack the characteristic of personality, however it may be transfigured in the reality.

This refashioned Christianity, accordingly, humanist and evolutionist as it will be, will yet be permeated and controlled by the consciousness of GOD as personal (which means a GOD transcending the process in which He is none the less inherent, for personality in us means that we too in our measure are conscious of a similar transcendence), and of Christ as the supreme manifestation of Him that has emerged in the process, and the medium of the true knowledge of GOD and Man in all their relationships with one another.

I cannot see how reinterpretation of our formularies on these lines can give us as our religion a Christianity that could be called 'reduced', unless it is by the quantity rather than the quality of its beliefs that the Christianity of our religion is to be measured.

For EU product safety concerns, contact us at Calle de José Abascal, 56–1°,
28003 Madrid, Spain or eugpsr@cambridge.org.

www.ingramcontent.com/pod-product-compliance
Ingram Content Group UK Ltd.
Pitfield, Milton Keynes, MK11 3LW, UK
UKHW020314140625
459647UK00018B/1874